THE COMPLETE GUIDE TO AUSTRALIAN SHEPHERDS

Kirsten Tardiff

LP Media Inc. Publishing

Text copyright © 2019 by LP Media Inc.

www.lpmedia.org

Publication Data

Kirsten Tardiff

The Complete Guide to Australian Shepherds ---- First edition.

Summary: "Successfully raising an Australian Shepherd Dog from puppy to old age" --- Provided by publisher.

ISBN: 978-1-67158-3-689

[1.Australian Shepherd Dogs --- Non-Fiction] I. Title.

This book has been written with the published intent to provide accurate and author-itative information in regard to the subject matter included. While every reasonable pre-caution has been taken in preparation of this book the author and publisher expressly dis-claim responsibility for any errors, omissions, or adverse effects arising from the use or application of the information contained inside. The techniques and suggestions are to be used at the reader's discretion and are not to be considered a substitute for professional veterinary care. If you suspect a medical problem with your dog, consult your veterinarian.

Design by Sorin Rădulescu

First paperback edition, 2019

TABLE OF CONTENTS

CHAPTER 1
About the Australian Shepherd

What is an Australian Shepherd?

"Even the most high-drive Aussie, if well bonded, will sit by your side when you are down or injured. They truly care about their pack and their people. I've never had an Aussie that had the same personality as any other Aussie. Each is quite unique."

Joan Fry
Bella Loma Kennels

*Photo Courtesy of
Karie King
Kicking K Australian Shepehrds*

Australian Shepherds are a member of the herding group of dogs, originally bred to work livestock. They have the toughness and agility to control rowdy cattle, but also the intelligence and discretion to move waddling, delicate ducks. They possess an incredible drive and desire to please their owner and are highly valued in performance sports such as Agility and Competitive Obedience. Aussies love what they do, and they do it all well. You'll never meet a more enthusiastic partner than an Australian Shepherd!

History of the Australian Shepherd

Their name is a bit of a misnomer - Aussies are an American-made breed. Basque shepherds in Europe developed a herding dog called the Pyrenean Shepherd that emigrated with them to Australia in the early 1800s. It is believed that there, the dogs were crossed with Border Collies and other breeds before migrating once again by the late 1800s, this time to the American west coast. These "little blue dogs" adapted to the wants and needs of farmers and ranchers in the American West, further perfecting the breed.

After World War II, the breed caught the American public's attention with the growing interest in the Western way of life. Aussies were often seen at rodeos performing tricks that entertained the crowds and soon became common sights at horse shows. They began appearing in movies and TV shows as well, further placing them in public view. A national breed club was established in 1957 and Aussies have enjoyed a steady rise in popularity worldwide ever since! In the United States, they rank as the 17th most popular breed of dog in 2019 per statistics from the American Kennel Club.

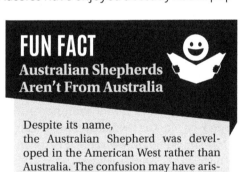

FUN FACT

Australian Shepherds Aren't From Australia

Despite its name, the Australian Shepherd was developed in the American West rather than Australia. The confusion may have arisen when Basque people brought the ancestor of the Australian Shepherd to the West Coast of America from Europe by way of Australia.

Today, most Aussies are beloved pets or successful competitors in various dog sports. Many still work on ranches and farms, helping to move and control livestock for their owners. This service often makes them indispensable, saving much time and effort on the part of their owners!

Physical Characteristics

Australian Shepherds were first formally recognized as a breed when the Australian Shepherd Club Of America (ASCA) was formed in 1957. Aussies did not enjoy recognition by the American Kennel Club (AKC) until 1990. Both breed clubs have a written breed standard that dictates what the ideal Australian Shepherd should look like and what temperament traits they should possess.

Aussies are most often medium-sized dogs between 35-55lbs and 18-23" tall. Contrary to popular belief, most breed registries do not recognize size variations (i.e. "Toy", "Miniature", "Standard"). Quality and work ethic are considered to be more important than size for an Aussie. A separate breed called the Miniature American Shepherd was recently developed from smaller than average Australian Shepherds for those who desire a similar, but a smaller dog.

Australian Shepherd body proportions are slightly rectangular, with medium bone size. Their heads are moderately broad, and the width and length of the skull should be equal to the length of the muzzle. They should have tight lips that never drool and almond-shaped, intelligent, expressive eyes. This skull and eye shape protect them from the flying hooves of agitated cattle, minimizing potential injuries. Their ears are set high on the head and fold forward (called a "button ear") or to the side (a "rose ear"), which keeps their ears clean and dry. Their bodies should be agile, athletic, and muscular; able to turn on a dime in a moment's notice. Aussies were bred this way to be able to safely and effectively work all day moving livestock. One of the most notable Aussie traits is a short bobtail, giving them their unique appearance and characteristic wiggle-butt when excited.

This breed should have medium-length hair and is double-coated; this means they have an undercoat of short, fine hair and a second layer of longer, somewhat coarser hair on the outside. While their coat is generally easy to care for, they shed heavily seasonally. Aussie coats come in four base colors – black, red, blue merle, and red merle. They can also have copper colored points, with or without white trim. A tricolor, or "tri", has the base coat color and both copper and white trim. A "bicolor" has only the base color and white trim, while a dog with a base color and copper but no white is called "red and copper", "black and copper", etc. A dog with no white or copper is "self-blue", self-red", etc. Aussies are also known for their large variety in eye colors, which can be any shade of brown, hazel/green, yellow/amber, or blue and include marbled eyes or eyes that are each different colors. Blue and marbled eyes are more common in merles due to their coat color.

Photo Courtesy of
Francine Guerra

Behavioral Characteristics

"Australian Shepherds are reserved with strangers. This does not mean shy or aggressive. This just means at first they are not everyone's best friend."

Heidi Mobley
Western Hills Australian Shepherds

Aussies were developed as an effective, versatile herding breed, but there is a surprising amount of variation between families and individuals. Most naturally display herding instincts, such as running after moving objects and weaving back and forth behind them, or nipping at the heels of humans, animals, or other dogs. While many Aussies naturally use their mouth to move and control whatever happens to be in motion around them - called "grip" - they aren't vicious and don't usually show unwarranted aggression. Australian Shepherds are not typically a noisy breed, but will bark to alert you if something is amiss.

This breed is extremely intelligent and likes to be mentally stimulated. They are smart enough to solve problems and manipulate their environment – their owners included – to entertain themselves and get what they want if you don't give them something to do. Aussies usually live to please their owners and love to be with their family. They have earned the nickname "Velcro dogs" for the way they become your shadow, often following you everywhere if allowed. Aussies generally don't tolerate overly stern training styles but thrive if given praise for a job well done. They typically have loads of energy and need daily physical exercise to keep them physically fit and avoid agitation due to pent up energy.

Aussies are usually reserved with strangers. They don't enthusiastically greet new people, rather treating them with cool indifference. They tend to guard their home and hearth against intruders, requiring lots of positive social interactions with new people from a young age to teach them to appropriately discern friend from foe. Some Aussies can atypically lack confidence and be shy or fearful. These dogs will need lots of training and careful socialization as they grow to help them become well-adjusted adults.

FUN FACT

Aussies Are Relatively New to the AKC

While some dog breeds have been registered with the American Kennel Club (AKC) for more than a century, the Australian Shepherd didn't join the AKC until 1993.

Photo Courtesy of
Amanda Watkins

Photo Courtesy of
Julie Caywood

Is an Australian Shepherd the Right Fit for You?

"Because the breed was created to assist the rancher in multiple duties, they have a strong connection to their master. This means they have one eye on you at all times and a desire to be at hand when needed."

Tina Beck
Goldcrest Aussies

Aussies present certain challenges to prospective owners. When you are trying to select a breed for your home, consider how much time you have, the activities you like to pursue, and what you really want in a new companion. Most dogs live an average of 12-14 years, which is a massive commitment. Take time to make sure an Aussie will bring you and your home joy, and that one would be happy living with you, too!

What kind of home do you have to provide for an Aussie? These dogs historically lived on massive ranches and farms, with plenty of room to live and work. While they do not necessarily require many acres or massive quantities of space, a medium to large size fenced yard is ideal. If you do not have a yard, will you be able to commit time to long walks, jogging, hiking, or trips to the park with your Aussie to meet his exercise requirements? Also, while traditionally Aussies were raised almost exclusively outside, farmers and ranchers spent the better part of their day working side by side with their dogs tending the livestock. An Aussie that is forced to

Photo Courtesy of Kelsey Dickerson

Photo Courtesy of
Chris Barnes

spend most of its time away from its family will be miserable. For most families today, that means an Aussie's place is inside the house. While they love to be outdoors, what an Aussie really wants most of all is to be with his favorite people.

Being very smart, an Aussie will need training. Typically, this involves at least a puppy kindergarten class to get started on the right foot. All dogs need clear boundaries and expectations, and Aussies in particular will thrive when given a "job" to do. This could mean teaching them tricks, competing in dog sports, helping you bring the sheep in for the night, or more. Don't expect an Aussie to be content sitting on the couch all day. You need to be willing to make time daily to do fun things with your Aussie and be willing to teach them what you expect from them. Thankfully, they are easy to train and willing students!

Aussies have a thick coat which requires weekly brushing for mainte- nance and even more frequently during periods of heavy shedding. If you can't tolerate fuzzy little tufts of hair on your clothes and floating across the floor, this may not be the breed for you! You must be willing to dedicate time to teaching a puppy to like grooming so that this isn't stressful later. Like any dog, Aussies' nails need regular trimming, teeth and ears need cleaning, and they need occasional baths to help keep their skin healthy and smelling pleasant. If you don't want to dedicate time to grooming your dog yourself, can you afford to take it to a professional groomer every 8 weeks?

Can you provide the space, exercise, and time an Aussie needs to become a happy, healthy member of your family? If not, you may want to reconsider bringing one of these dogs home. If the answer is yes, congratulations! You have chosen a versatile, intelligent, enthusiastic dog that will spend his days working to please you!

CHAPTER 2
Choosing an Australian Shepherd

If you've decided an Australian Shepherd is right for you and your family, now is the time to think about where you will get your new companion. This is no time to rush, no matter how excited you may be. Finding the best will require a little patience and some planning.

Buying vs. Adopting

There is a heated public debate over which is better – sourcing your companion from a breeder or a rescue. The real answer is neither! Each has pros and cons, and what may be right for one person won't be for another.

The advantages of buying from a responsible breeder include health tested parent dogs, health guarantees, and breeder support. Serious breed-

Photo Courtesy of Francine Guerra

ers spend a significant amount of time vetting their dogs in order to only produce the very best dogs. If the parents are consistent in the traits you are looking for, you will have a higher degree of confidence in what your puppy will grow up to be like. Good breeders guarantee the health of their puppies, standing behind them. They support new owners throughout the life of the dog and can quickly become your best information resource concerning your dog.

The main disadvantage of buying a puppy from a breeder is generally cost. Reputable

HELPFUL TIP
Adopting an Australian Shepherd

Many people fall in love with the looks and personality of Aussies but aren't prepared for the vast amount of exercise and mental stimulation the breed requires. As a result, there is a higher than average number of Australian Shepherds in shelters and rescue groups. Many "behavioral issues" are easily fixable with plenty of exercise and mental stimulation provided by working or participating in a dog sport like agility, so don't be afraid of adopting an Aussie if you're prepared to meet its needs.

breeders spend a significant amount of their own money to produce quality dogs, so oftentimes the prices they ask for their puppies can reflect that. Another disadvantage is that care must be taken to ensure you are buying from a reputable breeder (further discussed in the next section of this book). There are many irresponsible breeders. These can be avoided by carefully interviewing breeders and looking for recommendations from veterinarians or other professionals.

Rescues and shelters can be a great place to adopt your Aussie. Usually, rescue and shelter animals are already spayed or neutered and have been brought up to date on vaccinations and veterinary care. Most adoption fees are a fraction of the cost you would pay a breeder. Also, providing a home for an Aussie without one is a wonderful act of compassion! There are many good Aussies looking for loving homes through no fault of their own!

One of the disadvantages of adopting a dog from a rescue is that many have unknown histories, and some may need extra training and require empathy from their new owners while they adjust to a new life. Also, most dogs brought into rescues are over six months of age. If you specifically want a puppy, this may take time if you're looking at rescues.

How to Find a Reputable Breeder

Simply put, a reputable breeder is someone who puts the best interests of their dogs first. Conversely, someone that prioritizes monetary gain, or blue ribbons, or anything else over their dogs' well-being is likely not making responsible choices concerning their dogs' health and happiness and is not a responsible breeder.

Why is buying from a reputable breeder so important? While many people buy dogs from backyard breeders or puppy mills, this is a bad idea because irresponsibly bred dogs are far more likely to have serious health and temperament problems that make them ill-suited to be happy, long-lived companions. Some people end up buying a puppy from a bad situation to rescue it...however, while heart-breaking, this just adds to the problem. Puppy mills and backyard breeders continue to be a problem because people continue to buy from them. If we stop giving them an incentive to continue, they will cease to exist. If you find a breeder who has poor living conditions for their animals, the best course of action is to report them to authorities and pass them by. Don't enable this sad situation to continue!

Be aware that just because someone breeds two dogs to make puppies, this does not make them a reputable breeder. Amateurs can quickly run into genetic temperament and health problems if they don't know what they're doing. It is best to choose a breeder who uses tools like genetic and health screening, is very familiar with the pedigrees of the dogs they are working with, and has had years of experience in the breed. If they are a newer breeder (less than a decade in the breed), find out if they have a mentor to help guide them.

One of the best ways to find a reputable breeder is to talk to a professional. Your veterinarian, local professional dog trainer, or groomer are great places to start. You can also try asking people you know who have an Aussie you admire where they got theirs. Otherwise, most breeders have a website, so an internet search for Australian Shepherd breeders in your area may yield good results as well.

Most serious breeders do not have puppies available regularly – perhaps only one or two litters per year. If someone has puppies available constantly or is breeding multiple breeds or "designer" breeds, those are big red flags that the breeder is out to make a quick buck rather than to produce quality dogs. Never buy from a breeder that allows puppies to leave their mother and siblings before eight weeks old. Those last few weeks are a critical time for the puppy to learn how to interact with other dogs.

Ideally, begin looking for a breeder to work with about one year before you plan to bring a puppy home. This gives you time to select and get to know your breeder. Many people wait until the last minute to search for a puppy, and while you can find puppies available on short notice, you may have a more difficult time finding what you are looking for if you have something specific in mind.

Interviewing Breeders

"Choose a dog that fits your lifestyle. While Aussies come in many colors, they also can be medium to high energy. Do not pick an animal by its wrappings. You have to live with your new friend for its whole life. Most good breeders will guide prospective owners into picking the right temperament for their home."

Francine Guerra
Alias Aussies

Photo Courtesy of
Beverly Cogan

Once you have a few leads on breeders you may want to work with, you can start contacting them. A good breeder should be willing to talk with you and to answer your questions patiently and thoroughly. Be courteous when you are talking to a breeder – this is a time to get to know them, not interrogate them. Avoid someone who is impatient, avoids answering questions, or becomes defensive. By the same token, expect to be asked questions yourself. Breeders want to ensure that you are ready to properly care for a puppy, prepared for this particular breed, and will provide a safe and loving home; help them by answering their questions honestly. Some even have questionnaires for prospective owners to fill out.

If the breeder has a website, take some time to read through it carefully. This will save you time and save the breeder from having to answer questions repetitively. If the following information is not stated on their website, important questions to ask include:

- When is the next litter planned? (if they don't have anything currently available),
- What are the parent dogs for that litter like?
- What specific types of health testing do they do?
- What health issues have they seen in their dogs?
- How long have they been involved in the breed?
- If you are interested in doing a dog sport with your Aussie, does the breeder compete in the same sport successfully with their dogs?

Also, ask the breeder for a copy of their health guarantee or contract and the price range for their puppies.

You should also ask yourself some questions, such as whether the parent dogs are the type of Aussie you would like to own and whether the timing for when the puppies can go to their new homes works for you.

A breeder should be happy to set up a time to allow you to meet their dogs and see where they're living and how they are kept. Are the dogs clean and healthy? Is their environment clean, with fresh water available and toys for them to play with? Is there a way for them to be exercised regularly? How are the dogs with visitors? Do they accept you into the home and warm up to you readily, or do they act afraid or aggressive? If you can't see the breeder's home in person due to distance, are they willing to provide a few references from previous buyers? Avoid a breeder who refuses to allow you to visit or seems like they have something to hide.

Photo Courtesy of
Sonya Roberts and Luke Moorman

Many breeders will refer you to another if they don't have what you are looking for, or don't have anything available in the timeframe you are looking at. This can be a great way to establish a good connection. Their referral is usually to someone they trust and is often a compliment to you as well. If you are on several waiting lists, be sure to let the breeders know, and alert them if you have selected a puppy from elsewhere. Breeders often try to ensure they have homes lined up for most or all of the puppies before they're even born, and they appreciate being kept in the loop. Some breeders require a deposit to be kept on their waiting list, and these are generally non-refundable, as they want to be sure you are serious before holding a puppy for you.

Health Tests and Certifications

Good breeders utilize health testing for their dogs' welfare. At a minimum, the parent dogs should have had their hips screened for dysplasia, and their eyes examined by a veterinary ophthalmologist for genetic defects. Many breeders also use genetic tests or take x-rays of elbows, shoulders, and patellas to check for other orthopedic issues. However, more tests do not necessarily mean healthier puppies. Not all breeders test for all things because those issues may not be known to be a problem in their dogs' pedigrees. How a breeder uses the pertinent health information they've gathered is what is most important.

Unfortunately, some health issues – such as epilepsy and most autoimmune diseases or allergies – do not have a genetic test. These diseases are best avoided by taking care when breeding families of dogs together and waiting until a dog is two to three years old before breeding, since many problems appear by that age. Even parents who have been certified free of hip dysplasia does not guarantee they will never produce a puppy with hip dysplasia – it only reduces the risk.

Avoid breeders who only do a genetic test panel. While this is a great tool, it does not replace the necessity to screen eyes and hips for problems. By the same token, a "clear" genetic panel does not mean a healthier dog. For most genetic diseases that have a test, carrying one gene for the disease is harmless, and causes no problems for the puppies if bred to a mate who does not carry for the disease.

Breeder Contracts and Guarantees

In order to ensure a breeder is doing the best they can to produce healthy dogs, look for a health guarantee! Many people do not understand that a health guarantee is NOT a guarantee that your dog will never have a health problem; that would be an impossible thing to promise. What it is, is a guarantee that a breeder has done everything they know how to prevent a health problem from arising, and if it does happen anyway, they will stand behind their puppy and take responsibility.

There are two different types of guarantees – general health and genetic health. General health guarantees take effect the day you take your puppy home and are meant to cover any illnesses that could be deemed the breeder's fault. This includes parasites such as worms or coccidia, and viral or bacterial illnesses like parvovirus or kennel cough. This guarantee is short term – usually about three days – and requires that you take the puppy to the vet to confirm an illness. Usually a breeder will either take the puppy back for treatment and refund you, or allow you to keep the puppy and refund you for the veterinary expenses you incurred.

Genetic health guarantees, on the other hand, are meant to cover debilitating or life-threatening diseases or congenital disorders. These could be things like epilepsy, blindness, or hip dysplasia. These guarantees should extend at least two years, as most of these sorts of problems take that long to show up. Genetic health guarantees that only cover a puppy's first year of life are next to useless. Usually, a breeder will offer a refund for what you paid for the dog or offer a second puppy as a replacement. Be aware that some breeders avoid having to make good on this guarantee by adding a clause that you must return your dog if you want them to fulfill their part of the agreement, assuming that you would rather keep your dog and forfeit your replacement or refund. This is heartless, and best avoided.

Most breeders make a distinction between "pet" contracts, and "show/breeding" contracts. If you are only looking for a family pet, the contract should require that the dog not be bred, that you spay or neuter the dog within a certain time frame, and that the breeder be given first right of refusal if you ever decide you cannot keep the dog. If you are considering breeding or showing your dog, usually the contract requires that the breeder co-own the dog with you for a set period of time, that the dog must be shown or earn titles, and that they must have health testing requirements met before breeding. These clauses are all meant to protect the dog and are acceptable. Read contracts carefully – if you are uncomfortable or unsure about a certain aspect, ask the breeder why they have it and whether it is negotiable.

Choosing the Perfect Pup

"My number one factor would be temperament. The temperament of the parents does get passed down to their offspring. Having bred several generations of different bloodlines, I'm always amazed how personality traits run consistently in a bloodline."

Joanne Harvell
Canyon Lake Aussies

If you are working with an experienced breeder well before a litter is ready to leave home, oftentimes they will choose your puppy for you, or offer only a few for you to choose from – not the entire litter! While many people balk at the idea, breeders know their puppies best, and they have spent time getting to know you as well. They are concerned with making the best possible match between puppy and owner because they want you to succeed!

If you are given a few options to choose from, think about what your ideal Aussie puppy would be like. Many people think of color or gender first, and breeders will usually try to work with you to factor in color preferences, but there are other things that should factor in more heavily when making your decision.

Photo Courtesy of
Julie Caywood

What would your ideal puppy's personality be like? What energy level are you looking for? When visiting a litter to choose a puppy from, look for a confident puppy that is willing to interact with you. This does not necessarily mean choosing the most active holy terror in the bunch, either! Puppies that react with fear or avoid you are generally not the easiest companions. Ask the breeder to describe each puppy's personality, and choose the one best suited to your lifestyle and activity level. A less confident, more reserved puppy may be an okay fit for a retired couple, but a playful, active, outgoing puppy would likely suit a family with children best.

There is little real difference between genders if they are spayed or neutered. Males often tend to be somewhat slower maturing, and their neuter surgery is less invasive, less expensive, and faster healing than a female's spay.

Sometimes, breeders have retired adult dogs or older puppies they held back that they have decided to place into a new home so that they can ensure they don't keep too many dogs. If you don't have the time to start a puppy off on the right foot, this is a great option! These dogs have been raised by an Aussie expert and given the very best start in life. Many have had significant amounts of training and are used to grooming, traveling, and more. They have the rest of their lives ahead of them to spend with you, and all the hard work has been done. Many breeders don't openly advertise adult dogs, so it is worth inquiring.

Raising Multiple Puppies from the Same Litter

Raising two puppies is not an easy task. Many breeders will hesitate to allow two puppies from the same litter to go to the same home because it can be challenging. However, with some extra time and effort it can be done well. Ideally, it is best to choose a puppy from each gender, but two brothers or sisters can also work. Two of the same gender can be somewhat more likely to fight as they grow closer to maturity, so firm boundaries and early intervention when problems arise can help prevent problems down the road. Two puppies often adjust to their new home much faster, and can help keep each other entertained and exercised.

One of the main difficulties when raising two puppies is ensuring that each dog has one-on-one time. After the first week home, they should be crated separately so they have their own space. You must make extra time and effort to ensure that each puppy has outings away from its sibling for socialization. They need time separately with the family and for training sessions. If the puppies are never separated, this can cause them to become more bonded to each other than to their family. Separating them later on can cause severe anxiety. Training can be slower with two puppies as well. Two puppies also mean twice the expenses!

Carefully consider whether you have the time and resources to juggle two puppies before bringing both home. For most people, it is best to wait until the first puppy is over one year of age and more mature before adding a second.

Adopting an Australian Shepherd

"With rescues, my biggest tip is make sure it's a reputable rescue and the dog has been in rescue long enough that they can truly tell you what the dog is like. Some dogs come into rescue with zero history and the dogs typically do NOT come from responsible/reputable breeders."

Melonie Eso
WCK Aussies

Adopting a dog is a wonderful choice to make. Local animal shelters are a great place to start your search. However, you may have to wait a while for an Aussie to come in if you live in an area with a lower population. A second option would be a rescue specializing in Aussies or herding breeds. This is a great choice if you are looking for something very specific, as rescues often have foster homes lined up and take more time getting to know the dog, as well as finding the right placement for them. Many county or city-run shel-

Photo Courtesy of
Charles Donald Sinden Jr
Sinded Aussies

ters have very limited space and resources, and by necessity are more concerned with moving dogs than they are finding the "perfect placement".

Beware of rescue scams. Unfortunately, with the push to adopt pets, con artists pull at peoples' heartstrings and source puppies from puppy mills labeled as "rescues," then resell them. Avoid "rescues" that have almost exclusively puppies, offer registration papers on the puppies, or travel from place to place. When someone buys puppies from a puppy mill, this just encourages the mill to produce more puppies. While it is difficult to walk away from these situations, breaking the cycle is the only way to make it stop.

When choosing a rescue Aussie, be sure to take your time. While it is difficult to not want to save the first available Aussie that comes along, it is best to choose one that will suit your family and lifestyle. Does the dog get along with other dogs or pets, if you have them? Do you have children, and if so, would this dog be a safe and happy addition to your family? Does this Aussie have any ongoing medical needs, and can you afford to cover them? Are there any behavioral issues that need to be addressed, and if so, are you willing to commit the time and effort into correcting those behaviors? Most Aussies in rescues are great dogs that were just dealt a bad hand or need some training to become great companions.

Choosing the perfect Aussie for your home takes a lot of time and thought. However, making the right choice will ensure many years of joy for you, your family, and your new Aussie.

CHAPTER 3
Preparing Your Home for Your Australian Shepherd

"I recommend 'child proofing' your house. Puppies love wires especially those attached to chargers. Stair cases should be blocked off. Electric sockets plugged. Everything you would do for a toddler, do for your new puppy."

Francine Guerra
Alias Aussies

Photo Courtesy of
Amanda Gabriel

Photo Courtesy of
Rebecca Swyers

"Buy a crate for times you cannot supervise, remove cords and any furniture/shoes you find valuable."

Allison Lutterman
DreamWinds Aussies

You've settled on the perfect Aussie for your family and the day you get to bring it home is drawing close. There will be big changes coming for you, your family, any other pets, and your new dog. Being prepared can help make adjusting far easier! You'll need to take some time to walk through your home, yard, and any other spaces that aren't used to housing a dog or a new puppy, noting areas that contain safety hazards. Boundaries will need to be set for children and other pets as well. With a little work, you'll be ready to welcome your new Aussie into the family!

Dangerous Things That Dogs Might Eat

Dogs, and puppies in particular, like to explore the world with their mouths. Many emergency trips to the vet can be avoided if some care is taken in advance. Dangerous things dogs swallow include toxic human food, toxic plants, chemicals, human medications, and inedible items that cause intestinal blockages.

Human foods that are toxic to dogs include:

- Grapes and raisins
- Chocolate
- Avocados
- Onions
- Garlic
- Fruit cores
- Fresh yeast (in things such as bread dough)
- Caffeine and alcohol
- Large amounts of foods high in fat (like cheese, hot dogs, etc.)
- Sugar-free products containing Xylitol (candies, chewing gum)

Avoid giving table scraps to your dog, keep food items well out of reach, and secure kitchen trash cans with a tight lid or in a closed pantry to prevent your dog from getting access to these toxic things.

Photo Courtesy of Mikala Kempkers

There are numerous toxic plants. Keep houseplants well out of reach of your Aussie, or in a room they can't access. The more common houseplants that cause problems include:

- Ivy
- Jade
- Sago palm
- Elephant ear
- Dracaena
- Pothos
- Philodendron
- Dieffenbachia

- A few common toxic garden or landscaping plants include:
- Foxglove
- Lily-of-the-valley
- Daffodils
- Yew
- Hydrangea
- Holly

There are many more plants that can cause digestive upset or other toxic reactions. Research what plants you are gardening with and check with your veterinarian for toxicity if you aren't sure. Consider moving or replacing toxic plants, or putting up a stout barrier.

The most common chemicals ingested by dogs are antifreeze and rat poison, by far. Avoid using poison to control rodents if possible, and check areas where vehicles are parked regularly for leaks. Avoid using pesticides or herbicides anywhere near where your dog may come into contact with them. They often become exposed by walking through treated areas and subsequently licking their paws. Ensure cleaning products used indoors have had a chance to fully dry on surfaces before your dog is allowed in those areas, and that the containers are always kept in a secure cabinet. Never leave any containers of chemicals anywhere your dog may be able to reach them!

You should never give your dog human medication without veterinary approval. Certain medications - even over-the-counter painkillers or vitamins - can cause severe stomach ulcers, organ failure, or death. Keep medications in drawers or cabinets well out of reach of your dog to prevent accidental ingestion.

Indigestible items that cause intestinal blockages which often require surgery to remove are probably the most common dangerous things dogs eat. Choking hazards are also a concern. Avoid these problems by frequently walking through the house and yard picking up items that your dog could attempt to swallow. Socks, decorative landscaping rocks, and pieces of their own toys or children's toys are some of the more common culprits.

Photo Courtesy of
Sheila Rankin

Other Household Dangers

Other things that can pose a threat to your Aussie's safety include electrical cords, garbage, swimming pools, and toilets. Carefully hide or remove any exposed electrical wires or cables to avoid burns or electrocution risks. Swimming pools should be fenced off or located in an area that is otherwise inaccessible to your dog. Most dogs are great swimmers, but if your Aussie struggles to get out of the pool it can pose a drowning risk; especially for young puppies. Toilet lids should always be kept down – people don't want their dog drinking out of the toilet to begin with, but it can also be very toxic if you use cleaner tablets in the tank.

Preparing a Space for Your Dog Inside

Dogs need a safe, comfortable space they can call their own and relax in. Crates are perfect for this, as well as keeping your dog safe and assisting with housetraining. Choose a location or two to place a crate, preferably in a quiet area out of the way; a bedroom might be a good choice. Once your Aussie learns that the crate is his own safe space, he will often choose to nap in it or retreat to it of his own accord.

Restricting access to certain areas of the house at times is wise, particularly for young puppies that may find things to get into or are working on housetraining. Baby or pet gates are an easy, inexpensive way to accomplish this. Doors can be used but can easily be mistakenly left open if it is a frequently trafficked space. If the family is in the living room, you can gate off other areas of the house to keep them near you and out of trouble, and so on.

Very young puppies will not be able to hold their bowels and bladder for more than a few hours at a time. Depending on your availability to take them out to potty, you may want to set up a small pen or gate the puppy in your bathroom instead of using a crate. Place a couple pee pads on one side of the space and make sure the puppy has a few toys to play with. If your breeder raised your puppy with a wood pellet litter box this will also work very well. Complete housetraining will likely take a little longer with this method, but it is doable. You never want a puppy to be forced to soil his crate or somewhere else in the house!

Photo Courtesy of
Reese Slater

Preparing Outside Spaces

Yards give your Aussie a convenient place to relieve himself and to exercise. If the area is smaller than 20'x20', you probably won't have enough space to allow your dog to really burn energy and will need to consider walking or jogging to keep him fit. Dog urine can burn grass over time, so you may want to teach your Aussie to go in one corner of the yard to minimize the damage and water the grass more frequently there.

One of the most important parts of a safe outside space for your Aussie is a good fence. Chain-link, wood panel, picket style or some privacy-type fences should be sufficient. They should be at least four feet tall. Some Aussies can easily jump or scale four-foot fences, so bear this in mind. With supervision and a little training, if needed, it will work for most. Check for holes your Aussie could squeeze through or slip under. Ensure gates can be

HELPFUL TIP

Childproof Your Home

Between their high energy levels and extreme intelligence, Aussies will fight boredom by finding creative ways to get into trouble when left alone. To keep your Australian Shepherd safe, you may need to childproof your home even more carefully than you would for a toddler.

securely latched and are never left open. Avoid invisible fences that use a buried wire and an electronic collar to train your dog. While some owners swear by these and have managed to avoid any incidents, these fences are extremely unreliable. Many dogs have been lost, injured, or killed because of invisible fence failures. Many Aussies are smart enough to figure out if they bolt over the line, the corrections from the collar stop. It can take just one mistake for a tragic accident to occur.

Outdoor shelters like dog houses are unnecessary if your Aussie spends most of his time with the family indoors. Some shade from a tree or canopy is appreciated on hot summer days while they play and exercise outside. Chaining your Aussie is never a good idea – there is a high risk of strangulation or getting tangled, and if you don't have a fence your dog has no way to protect itself from ill-intentioned humans and strange dogs.

If you live in a climate where you get snow or ice and need to use salt to clear steps and walkways, be sure to use pet-safe salt. Regular road-type salt can burn or irritate your Aussie's paw pads and can be toxic if ingested. If you walk or jog with your Aussie on the side of the road, consider putting dog booties on his feet or using a paw wax, then ensure you wash them when you return.

Preparing Children and Your Current Pets

"The herding instinct can be difficult to handle, especially around kids. The instinct is to chase anything that moves and nipping can be included in this behavior. Kids should be taught to stop, or stand like a statue when herding kicks in. Sometimes it's best to put the dog away when there are many triggers for this behavior. Redirection to a toy can also be beneficial, as is training impulse control."

Gayle Silberhorn
Big Run Aussies

Photo Courtesy of Pam Brauer

It's great to see a bond develop between kids and the family dog. You can help strengthen this bond and prevent accidents from occurring with some ground rules for your children. Provide your Aussie with a space of his own – ideally a crate – and ensure your kids know that this area is off limits to them. This way, your Aussie has a place to retreat to and relax as needed without being disturbed. Children should also be taught to never, ever pull your Aussie's ears, hair, or lips, to climb on him, hang on him, or strike him. There should be an absolute zero-tolerance policy in place that is understood before you ever bring your Aussie home. To expect your dog to put up with this kind of behavior from children is completely unfair and asking for a bite to occur. It is not cute and it is not acceptable. No one likes their space invaded or to be used as a toy or punching bag! Children should also be included in the care and training of your Aussie. This teaches them responsibility and will deepen the bond between them.

If you have another dog at home, make sure you don't have any serious problem behaviors that are left unresolved before bringing another into the mix. Your new Aussie can and likely will pick up bad habits from your current dog - then you'll have double the trouble. Also, make sure your current dog has a crate or a bed of his own and a place to retreat from a new puppy, especially if your current dog is elderly. A young puppy can be overwhelming to an older dog. They'll both be happier if they have access to their own spaces!

Most cats can take a while to warm up to a new addition - sometimes even months. Before bringing home your new Aussie, make sure your cats have a safe, high place to get to easily, like a cat tree or similar. This is especially helpful if located in the most frequented area of the home near a gated off doorway, as it allows your cat to access its space and permits the cat to observe the new addition safely without having to cross a room. Keep litter boxes and your cat's food dish in a place you are absolutely certain your Aussie can't reach.

Pocket pets, birds, and exotics are best kept separate from your Aussie for safety. Aussies will not usually try to intentionally hurt small animals, but they are fragile and even playful gestures can cause accidental harm. Ensure their food and bedding are stored in dog-proof containers and keep their cages or habitats out of reach of your Aussie.

Attention to detail is the key to making your home a safe and welcoming place for your new addition. Being prepared ahead of time will help make this an easy transition for your Aussie and your family! Now, you are almost ready to bring them home.

CHAPTER 4
Bringing Home Your Australian Shepherd

"Buy a crate for crate training, a pen to restrict their freedom, plenty of toys, training treats, and a good quality dog food. Plan to attend a puppy kindergarten class."

Joanne Harvell
Canyon Lake Aussies

The day you have been waiting for is finally approaching - you have a date set to bring your Aussie home! Now is the time to make the final preparations. This includes having a routine in place (especially for puppies), gathering the last few supplies, choosing a veterinarian and making the first vet appointment. These last few days are filled with excitement and the anticipation that adding to the family brings!

Photo Courtesy of Kayla Spangler

Photo Courtesy of
Josh Tuggle

The Importance of Having a Plan

"Everyone in the home needs to know what the rules are going to be for the dog and all follow these rules. The rules that are set in the household needs to be the same rules as the dog grows up. So think of these rules as for an adult dog, and not just a puppy."

Heidi Mobley
Western Hills Australian Shepherds

Having a set plan or routine in place before you bring your Aussie home will help him to adjust to his new life with you more quickly. Dogs are creatures of habit and thrive on a schedule. Choose a set time for meals each day – this makes potty training for puppies significantly easier as you will know when they need to go out. Also, who in the family will feed your Aussie? Assigning the task will help prevent accidental missed or doubled meals. This is a great chore for older children to help teach responsibility

FUN FACT

AKC Ranking

As of 2017, the Australian Shepherd is the 17th most popular dog in the United States.

and to help them bond with your new addition.

Potty breaks should always be set for after meals, first thing in the morning, and before bedtime at the very least. Puppies will need more frequent breaks. Will someone need to stop in at home during the day to let the puppy out for the first few weeks until he is older? Another thing to keep in mind is what happens in the event of an emergency. Who is responsible for ensuring your Aussie is let out and cared for? Do you have a trustworthy friend or neighbor who is willing and prepared to help if necessary?

Supplies to Have Ready

"If you are taking in a puppy, you will find they are very proud of their teeth and may use them at inappropriate times. This does not mean your puppy will be biting aggressively as an adult, it just means the breed has developed a use for their bite in herding and it is natural for them to hone that skill early in life."

Tina Beck
Goldcrest Aussies

Pet supply shopping sprees are loads of fun! Here is a list of things you will likely need:

- Crate - 36" wire with a divider panel is ideal
- Large dog bed, preferably washable and made of durable materials
- Nylon or leather flat buckle collar and 6' leash
- A large variety of safe, durable, appropriate toys
- Food and water bowls
- Dog food – ensure that you either get the same brand they are currently eating, or a small bag of their current food to switch over to your chosen food
- Waste disposal supplies, such as waste baggies

Photo Courtesy of
Amanda Bocek

- Pet stain cleaners in case of accidents
- Metal pin brush, undercoat rake, pet nail trimmers, and a dog shampoo for grooming

When purchasing items for your new Aussie, keep quality and safety in mind. A $10 pet bed may not hold up to puppy teeth, but a more expensive and easily washable design intended to resist chewing probably will! We all love a good deal, but sometimes a low price is too good to be true and then you will be throwing money away.

Toys especially should be of good quality. Choose a variety of styles – rubber, nylon, and denim for example are generally tough and well-made. Ensure you choose toys that can't be easily shredded and eaten, and that are big enough not to be a choking or swallowing hazard– usually "medium" to "large" sized toys work well. Avoid cooked or smoked bones as these can often splinter and cause serious digestive harm or blockages. Also avoid rawhide bones, which are made with chemicals that can be harmful to your Aussie and when eaten, can often cause tummy upsets.

You can often find crates for a good deal available second hand on sale sites or at garage sales. Ensure the crate is in good repair, has an undamaged pan or tray, and preferably a divider panel so that you can start smaller for a puppy and increase the space as your dog grows!

The Ride Home

The big day is here! Whether your Aussie is nearby, a road trip away, or an airline flight away there are some things you can do to prepare the dog. For starters, make sure you plan plenty of potty breaks for road trips over an hour long. Young puppies may need breaks as often as every couple of hours. Usually they will drift off to sleep after a bit but if they wake up - pull over! Have plenty of cleaning supplies on hand, including paper towels, pet stain remover and waste disposal baggies. Ideally, ask the breeder or pet rescue not to feed your Aussie within 2 hours of the time you pick him up. This will minimize the risk of car sickness or accidents on the ride home. Do bring water and a bowl, but only offer it during a rest stop, and give your Aussie at least 20 minutes to relieve himself after drinking before taking off again.

The safest place for your dog to travel is in a crate; dogs are often thrown out of vehicles when car accidents occur because they are loose and have nothing to stop their momentum. Your crate should allow just enough room for your Aussie to turn around and lie down comfortably, no more.

Photo Courtesy of Kayla Guzman

You can line the crate with absorbent towels and place a few toys inside to help keep the dog occupied.

Occasionally it may be necessary to fly your Aussie to you. The breeder or rescue generally makes all of the arrangements, purchases the airline ticket and crate on your behalf, and obtains the necessary health papers. When you are picking up your Aussie at the airport, you will usually have to prove your identity and sign paperwork provided by the airline. As soon as you receive your dog, take him out for a potty break and offer him a drink of water. Sometimes flying can be a little stressful, so your Aussie may act uncertain at first. Speak softly to him while he adjusts after the flight and be patient. Most will warm up quickly, and some will take it all in stride!

The First Night Home

"Puppies test out their new environment and boundaries with chewing, scratching, tugging and digging. Everything is potentially edible. Everything is potentially reachable. The smarter the puppy, the more trouble the puppy can potentially get into. Exercise their mind and body as much as possible."

Francine Guerra
Alias Aussies

The first night can sometimes be the hardest. Everyone in the family is likely very excited, but try not to overwhelm your new Aussie. Remind children to be calm and gentle with him. Avoid introducing your Aussie to any new pets the first night, as it is best to give him some time to adjust to his new home. Some may not seem very interested in you at first, but don't take it personally – they are still figuring out what happened to their world and trying to make sense of it all. New arrivals are often more reserved the first few days which is very normal.

From the very first night, your Aussie should sleep in his kennel as that is "his place", his bed. Puppies, in particular, will often cry the first night, especially if they are not used to a crate. Stand firm. If you let him out every time he cries, your puppy will quickly learn that screaming at three in the morning is rewarded. However, puppies under 12 weeks old will usually need to go potty sometime during the night. If your puppy awakens you after sleeping quietly for a few hours, do take him outside. Allow him to do his business, but resist playing with him. As soon as he is finished, he should be placed back in his crate. He will very likely cry for a little while before finally going back to sleep. Puppies thrive on consistency, and if you are consistent and firm from the beginning, this stage will pass quickly.

HELPFUL TIP
Buy Pet Insurance Early

While Australian Shepherds aren't prone to quite as many health problems as some other breeds, their intelligence and energy levels can lead to swallowed foreign objects or escapes that result in being hit by a car. Most pet insurance plans have waiting periods and exclude preexisting conditions, so the best time to sign up is as soon as you bring your Aussie home.

Remember to follow your planned routine from the very first night onward. This will greatly help your Aussie adjust to your home and family. If you find you need to make an adjustment to the routine, that's ok! Just stick to any changes and maintain consistency.

Introducing Your Australian Shepherd To Your Other Pets

Allowing your Aussie to meet the other furry family members should be done in a structured way to try to start everyone off on the right foot. If you have more than one other dog, introduce them to your Aussie one at a time. Introductions should be done in an open, neutral area. Hallways for example are a tight space that may make animals feel trapped. A living room or yard are ideal. No food or toys should be present as some dogs can feel threatened and possessive.

If one dog is very exuberant and the other is not, place that dog on a leash. Allow the dogs to calmly meet and watch their body language. Sniffing, a relaxed expression, fast tail wagging, and play bows are all excellent signs. Stiff bodies, yawning, licking lips, and hair standing along their backs are a sign that tension is brewing and the dogs should be separated for a while. Puppies will often lick and nibble the chins of adults or roll over on their backs, which is perfectly normal. If the adult dog growls at the puppy or snarls, then stops when the puppy backs off, do not correct or scold this behavior. This is how the older dog is teaching the puppy to be respectful. Actual biting, or continuing to snarl or "lay out" the puppy even when he has retreated or rolled onto his back should be stopped immediately. Intervene by taking the older dog by the collar with a firm but calm "No!", and remove them from the puppy.

47

If the introductions have a rocky start, don't give up. Preventing an actual fight from occurring and allowing the dogs to spend time near one another, even if they aren't interacting, can usually smooth over any tensions. Try walking the dogs a few times per day near each other but not close enough to touch. You can also place a gate between two rooms with a dog in each so that they can see and even interact somewhat with each other, but can easily retreat if they wish. If after 10-14 days you have not been able to fully integrate your Aussie into the household with your other dogs, contact an animal behaviorist for help.

Give your Aussie and your other dog or dogs time away from each other at first, even if introductions have gone well, especially if your other dog is elderly. A puppy can be stressful on an older dog at first, and it will appreciate some time away from puppy shenanigans! You can accomplish this by rotating each dog's time out during the day, with one in their crate with a special toy or treat while the other has time out.

Aussies generally get along very well with cats, however, the feeling is not always mutual! Never force an interaction between your Aussie and your cat. This will likely cause a great deal of stress for your cat and can quickly start them off on the wrong foot. Allow your cat space to observe from a distance and greet your Aussie on its own terms. If your Aussie tries to chase or pounce on the cat, give a firm but calm "No!" or "Ah-ah!", take him by the collar, and walk away from the cat. Redirect the dog to a toy instead, and reward him with a treat or a little game of tug when he leaves the cat in peace.

Choosing a Vet and the First Vet Visit

Choosing a reputable veterinary clinic is an extremely important step to set your Aussie up for a lifetime of good health. Ask around to see who others in your area recommend. Don't be afraid to call and ask questions, or to visit the clinic in person before taking your Aussie in. The clinic should be clean and well-managed. The waiting room should not be overly crowded, and waiting times to see the vet should not be more than 15-20 minutes from your appointment time unless there is an emergency patient brought in to the clinic.

When choosing a veterinarian to work with, ideally they should be willing to answer your questions patiently and thoroughly. They should be kind and gentle with your dog. While the vast majority of veterinarians are in their field because they love what they do and they have your Aussie's best interest at heart, a minority of clinics are more profit-motivated. Remember, you are your dog's advocate. You are the one who must ultimately decide what is best for him. It is in your dog's best interest for you to be an informed, active participant in your dog's healthcare plan.

Don't forget to be respectful of your veterinarian's time and expertise. Show up to your appointments on time, thank them for their services, and pay without grumbling. Many clinics offer some of the same medical tests and procedures that human hospitals do. This equipment is extremely expensive to purchase and maintain, yet veterinary clinics only charge a fraction of what human hospitals do. Do not assume your vet is out to rob you.

Your first vet visit should ideally be scheduled a few weeks in advance of your Aussie's arrival. Set the appointment for about 48hrs after you bring the dog home. Most breeders have a short term general health guarantee, and if your Aussie falls ill before coming to you, you want to document that to be able to fall under that guarantee. Bring all veterinary records with you to the clinic.

At the appointment, bring a few small treats to make the experience enjoyable for your Aussie, especially puppies. Keep your Aussie on a leash and close by you; many dogs are not enthused about vet visits, so now is not the time for introductions with other dogs. The receptionist will usually have you weigh your dog, you will wait a few minutes, then you will be called into an exam room. You'll be asked questions about your Aussie's current health status and what you are feeding him. Like many other herding breeds, your Aussie may be sensitive to Ivermectin and certain other medications, so make certain you inform the vet. After all this, and usually another short wait, the veterinarian will see you. Your dog's eyes, ears, teeth, genitals, and abdomen will be examined and he will have his temperature taken. He may also receive any necessary core vaccines. Now would be a good time to ask any questions you may have for your vet!

Photo Courtesy of Hunter B. Martin

Photo Courtesy of
Erik Heise

Puppy Classes

"I ask people to make dog training their hobby as an instructor who is familiar with herding breeds can identify the dog's body language and help guide the handler on a path of success. The time and money spent in training classes will be one of your best investments."

Tina Beck
Goldcrest Aussies

Puppy obedience classes are a fantastic, fun way to bond with your Aussie puppy and teach him manners. Start your puppy in a class and with training in general as soon as possible. Never wait until your puppy is older! By six months of age or older, if misbehavior and shenanigans have been allowed to go on for so long, this behavior will have become a set pattern. Begin to teach your Aussie when he is a little sponge, not a hard-headed, wild teenager that has gotten away with naughtiness for months!

Contact the local kennel club in your area to see when their next puppy kindergarten class is scheduled. Usually these are held once per week and run for four to eight weeks. Ask how long the instructor has been teaching and what their experience in dogs has been. Classes should be relaxed, informative, and structured. They should discuss basic socialization, teach you how to start your puppy's basic obedience training, and offer advice for manners training or misbehavior. Aussies in general, and puppies in particular, succeed most with positive reinforcement-based training. This method uses treats, praise, and toys to reward your dog for a job well done, as opposed to correction-based training that uses force or punishment when they do something wrong.

You will need to set aside time each week to train your puppy between classes. Usually instructors will do a review at the beginning of class the following week to see if you are making any progress, and address any struggles you have been having. While most of the training is done at home, the feedback you receive from an experienced trainer each week at class will be an extremely valuable asset to help you succeed with your puppy!

Welcoming your Aussie home is a special and exciting time for your family, and being prepared will make it a good experience for your Aussie, too! Stick to your routine, find a great veterinarian and training class, and take plenty of time to enjoy and bond with your new family member!

CHAPTER 5
Housetraining

Housetraining is probably the least exciting part of dog ownership, but one of the most important. There is nothing more frustrating than your home being used as a toilet! Many dogs are given up to a shelter because their owners did not housetrain them properly. Avoid problems early on by starting off on the right foot!

Options for Potty Training

There are several options for potty training. The first, and most common, is to teach your Aussie that he must relieve himself outside. This requires that you ensure he is taken outside often enough that he does not have the opportunity to have an accident in the house. Most dogs can fairly quickly make the connection if you are consistent and vigilant. Usually a grassy area in a yard or park is ideal, but if you do not have access to grass, it may take your new dog some time to learn to relieve himself on concrete or dirt.

Another option more popular with toy breeds are absorbent housetraining pads or litter boxes. These are ideal for young puppies if you cannot be home to let them out frequently enough the first month while you are away at work during the day. They can be used for adult dogs, but the amount of waste is larger, so the trays and boxes must be larger and will become heavily soiled rather quickly. The odor can also quickly become a turnoff.

HELPFUL TIP
Crate Training

Crate training isn't just helpful for house-training but is crucial to ensure the safety and happiness of your Australian Shepherd down the road. Even if you don't plan to crate your dog when you leave it home alone, your Aussie may still encounter a crate or kennel down the road, for example, at the groomer or vet's office, and you don't want your pet to be afraid of the situation. That's why crate training your puppy is crucial.

A third option is training your dog to use a doggy door, where he has access to a run or yard at all times. This is the ultimate in convenience over the long term. However, this setup is not viable for all homes, and measures should be taken to ensure the safety of your dog outside while you are away from home.

The First Few Weeks

"Don't set them up for failure. Watch for signs like sniffing the ground and LOTS of praise when they go outside. Also teaching them to potty while on a leash is a good idea."

Melonie Eso
WCK Aussies

Photo Courtesy of
Sheila Romanski.

Consistency and preventing mistakes are the keys to housetraining your Aussie properly. After you have decided how you want to housetrain your Aussie, you need to know the key times he will need to relieve himself, and what the signs are.

As a general rule, puppies need to eliminate after any activity. This means immediately after waking up, eating or drinking, after approximately 20 minutes of playing, or right after training sessions. Adult dogs should be allowed time to relieve themselves several times per day. Usually first thing in the morning, immediately before turning in for the night, immediately after meals, and at least once sometime during the day. Signs your dog needs to be taken out or shown to the potty area are circling and sniffing the floor, and whining. Some catch on quickly and try to let you know by staring at you, or sitting in front of the door.

Puppies can only hold their bowels and bladder for one hour for every month of age. So, a two month old puppy should only be expected to wait for a maximum of two hours. If you cannot make it home often enough to allow your puppy to relieve itself, either arrange for a friend or neighbor to take the puppy out for you, or set up a small playpen with housetraining pads or a litter box for the first month or two. It is unacceptable for a puppy to be forced to try to hold it in a crate while you are away. He will inevitably have an accident, and the more often this happens, the more ingrained that behavior will become. Set your puppy up for success, not failure!

Photo Courtesy of
Jessica Graf

Photo Courtesy of
Kirstie Kettleton

Rewarding Correct Behavior

When your Aussie relieves himself in the appropriate area, throw a little party! A small treat and happy, controlled praise for a job well done will further reinforce that this is the behavior you want. You may also choose to "mark" the behavior with a command, like "go potty!" before giving the praise and reward. This can be useful if you need your dog to eliminate at specific times on command.

If you come across a mess in the house, you can be frustrated – but only at yourself. Your dog does not yet grasp the concept. You are at fault for allowing your dog to be set up to fail. Do not punish your dog, do not yell and do not rub his nose in it. A dog does not have the level of intelligence to connect its previous action to the current punishment. All you are doing is frightening your dog and damaging its relationship with you. However, if you catch him in the act, a firm but calm "No!" or "Ah ah!" can interrupt them. Immediately take him outside or to his pads, allow him to finish, then reward him when he finishes his business in the appropriate place! And next time – prevent it before it happens!

Be sure to use an enzymatic cleaner if your Aussie makes a mistake in the house. Dogs tend to reuse areas that smell like waste, so the last thing you want is for him to be encouraged to use that area again!

Crate Training for Housetraining Use

"Keep their area small initially. They should either be under your direct supervision or they should be in a crate or small pen. Period. If they're allowed too much freedom and allowed to roam, they will have accidents. It's a lot easier to do it right from the beginning than to have to back up and undo bad habits."

Joanne Harvell
Canyon Lake Aussies

Crates are the single most useful tool you will have to housetrain your Aussie. Dogs generally do not like to be around their own waste, and they will not soil where they sleep. When their crate becomes their den, they will learn to hold their bowels and bladder to avoid making a mess. Crates must be of the appropriate size – your dog should have just enough room to turn around and lie down comfortably, no more. If the crate is too large, the puppy will usually just potty in one end and sleep in the other! As noted earlier, many wire crates come with removable divider panels. This way, you can buy one adult size crate and just block off the extra space, increasing the size as the puppy grows.

You can use blankets, beds, or pads in the crate, but make sure they are durable, washable, and not being eaten! Some Aussies are determined chewers, so do not feel bad if your puppy must have a bare floor for safety's sake. Fabric shreds can cause life-threatening intestinal blockages if swallowed. Once the puppy shenanigans and teething have passed, you can try adding some bedding again.

To begin crate training, you need to teach your Aussie that the crate is his space and is a good, safe place. Always feed meals in the crate to help build that positive association. Designate special treats and toys for only while he is in the crate. Many rubber toys are made to allow you to stuff them with some treats or paste.

Make sure your Aussie has plenty of time outside of the crate. Dogs can become bored, and what should be a special space can become a prison. Crates should ideally be used at night, while your dog is home alone, and during times when he absolutely cannot be supervised. You must make time to keep an eye on mischievous puppies and frequently allow them time out to play and be with the family. Crates are great tools, but do not misuse them!

Playpens and Doggy Doors

Play pens and doggy doors can be great tools to help housetraining. Young puppies can be placed in a small playpen with a tray or litter box during times while you are away for several hours. This is especially useful if you can use whatever the breeder of your Aussie used for the puppies, as your dog will already be trained to use it. If you decide to use a litter box, choose a litter that is nontoxic. Various pellets are usually acceptable. However, some puppies are bound and determined to eat the litter. If you see this behavior, it is best to avoid any potential health problems and choose pads or another method instead.

Doggy doors are great if you have to be away from home during the day. Ensure the door is of an appropriate size; a 24" door should cover even the largest of Aussies. To teach him to use it, start with the flap off the door. Have another person call your Aussie through the door and reward him when he gets to the other side. Do this back and forth several times until your Aussie can manage it easily. Next, put the flap on the door and do the same thing. You may need to lift the flap a little bit at first. Slowly reduce the amount you are lifting the flap until he can push through it on his own in both directions.

Photo Courtesy of
Julie Caywood

If you are using a doggy door as a potty training method, first ensure the area the dog has access to on the other side is completely safe. The area should be fenced off and inaccessible to other dogs or wild animals, and gated or locked to prevent other people from reaching your dog. Next, set up a small pen on the inside of the house surrounding the doggy door. This area should be just large enough for the dog to lie down and be comfortable. After a few weeks, you can remove the pen and just gate off that room of the house, and he should continue to relieve himself outside.

Leaving Your Dog Home Alone

In a perfect world our dogs would always be with us everywhere we went, but unfortunately that is not reality! Your Aussie will spend time home alone at some point, and it is important to ensure that he is safe and comfortable while you are away. Generally, the best and safest place for your Aussie while he is home alone is in the crate. This is especially true for puppies. If a fire starts in your home and firemen in their gear and masks go in to try to save your Aussie, imagine how terrifying a sight that would be in a dog's eyes! He is likely to cower under a bed or run away from rescuers rather than allow himself to be caught. If he is in the crate, on the other hand, the firemen can lift or drag the crate to safety or reach in to take their collar. Besides the potential for fire risk, homes can be a dangerous place for

Photo Courtesy of
Lisa Ricard

puppies especially. Anything that can be chewed and swallowed probably will be, and no matter how well you think you puppy-proofed your home, he will likely find something!

If you do not want to use a crate, the next best bet is the doggy door system, playpen, or blocking them into a carefully proofed room. A mudroom or bathroom is usually ideal for the latter as long as shoes are picked up or toilet lids are left down! Ensure no cords or small items are within reach. Adult dogs can usually be trustworthy loose in the home if they haven't chewed on anything not their own recently, although some dogs have mild separation anxiety and can become destructive...these dogs actually often prefer the security of a crate!

If you are consistent and minimize accidents, you can usually have your Aussie fairly well housetrained within a few weeks. You will still need to ensure young puppies are taken out often enough and have a safe and appropriate space to be while you are away from home, but soon your hard work will pay off and you will have a thoroughly housetrained companion! This is one of the most important things you will ever train your dog to do, as no one likes to step in dog messes on the floor (including the dog)!

CHAPTER 6
Socializing with People and Animals

"I suggest taking the pup to places with people, noises, and other dogs under control, constantly varying their experiences. Never should a pup be forced. The best thing to do is to move back to where the pup is comfortable, give high praise and rewards and slowly move closer to things, people or places that they are not comfortable with. This may take a long time but slow and steady, even over a long period of time, pays higher rewards than pushing a pup in a situation they are not comfortable with."

Joan Fry
Bella Loma Kennels

Photo Courtesy of
Tania Gomez Ayala

Socialization is the concept of exposing your Aussie to a variety of positive stimuli, so that he can become accustomed to the things he may encounter in everyday life and take it all in stride. This includes greetings with a variety of people, taking him to new places, over many different surfaces, introducing him to other dogs, as well as exposing him to new sights and sounds. There is a right way and a wrong way to go about proper socialization.

Importance of Good Socialization

"Get them around as many other animals as you can. Allow them to understand that other animals and dogs are not always a threat. Anything an Aussie is not exposed to regularly when their young has the potential to be something they are afraid of as an adult. And fear leads to biting and fighting."

Joanne Harvell
Canyon Lake Aussies

HELPFUL TIP

Aussies Will Herd Anything, Including Children

Australian Shepherds were born to herd sheep, and they will use that instinct on anything that moves. Without livestock available, they will attempt to herd children, pets, people on bicycles, cars, and more. This may involve nipping at the heels of your children, so it's crucial to teach your puppy early on that nipping at humans is not acceptable.

Socialization is a crucial part of forming a well-rounded Aussie. Ideally, this should happen during the "critical socialization period" of the first 16 weeks of a puppy's life. During this time, puppies are essentially little sponges and adapt more readily to new experiences. Usually breeders begin this process in their own home from the day the puppies are born. Touching and handling the puppies, grooming them, exposing them to the sights and sounds of a home environment, and welcoming visitors are the very early basics. Many breeders also use various tools and programs to expose the puppies to new experiences each week as they grow!

After a puppy leaves the place it was born, socialization should continue. Puppies should be exposed to all sorts of surfaces – wood, carpet, tile and laminate floors, grass, dirt, gravel, and sand-covered ground. Encourage him to climb hills, tree stumps, and stairs. Take him to a new place each week, and make it a positive experience! Never force or pressure a puppy to interact with something he is unfamiliar with. While puppies readily remember positive experiences, they will also remember frightening and negative experiences as well. It is your responsibility to protect your puppy from a bad experience! Bad impressions can be incredibly difficult to undo once they have been made.

The consequences of a lack of socialization can often become apparent as a puppy grows into an adult. He may be hesitant to approach new people or dogs or might avoid walking across unfamiliar surfaces and shy away from or bark at strange objects. He may struggle to adapt to changes in his environment. Similar problems can be seen with a dog that has had a bad experience with something specific – if your Aussie was attacked by another dog, he may now fear interactions with other dogs, or even just dogs that look like the one that attacked him. A situation like this can take months of work to resolve!

Socializing with Other Dogs

"Do not force your Aussie into relationships, let them take their time and make the first step."

Adriana Plum
Turkey Run Australian Shepherds

Shaping your Aussie's interactions with other dogs is key to setting up a good foundation with dog-dog relations. Most Aussies are actually fairly dog-neutral; they will love their housemates and may make a few close doggy friends when properly acquainted, but they will be indifferent to most they meet on the street. Don't feel like your dog must love every other dog instantly! Most dogs actually fall into the dog-neutral category, and the minority truly love all other dogs. Really, this is not so different from human interpersonal relationships – you probably don't run up to every person you meet, throw your arms around them, and demand to be best friends, do you?

When introducing your Aussie to another dog, first ask the other owner for their permission. Some dogs feel very threatened by strange dogs and become aggressive as a way to defend themselves. If they decline your offer, that is ok – they are doing what is best for their dog. If you have their approval, allow the dogs to greet and sniff. They should not be acting wildly. Good signs are sniffing, relaxed expressions, fast tail wagging, and play bows. If one dog is growling, trying to retreat, curling his lips, or his hair is standing on end, calmly separate the two dogs immediately to prevent a fight from breaking out.

Photo Courtesy of Hope Bailey

Introducing puppies to other dogs should be done cautiously and in a controlled way. Older puppies can often play too rough with young puppies, so in most situations this is probably best avoided until the younger puppy is a little older. When socializing your puppy with an adult dog, be absolutely certain that the older dog is safe and tolerant of puppies before allowing them to meet.

Interactions With Other Pets and Livestock

You can also expose your Aussie to other animals. This is especially important if you own livestock or ever want to herd with your Aussie. Safety should always be kept at the forefront of your mind for both your dog and the other animals. Large animals like cattle and horses can be a hazard for your Aussie. A well-aimed kick can easily kill or injure them.

Aussies rarely will intentionally harm another animal. However, most will instinctually try to move or chase other animals, which can stress them or cause them to panic and accidentally harm themselves. Most introductions are best begun with a fence between to see how your Aussie will react. If he is fearful or becomes overly excited, move farther away until he is calm, then move closer again. Offer praise for calm, confident behavior. If you eventually want a fence-free encounter, make sure you have an absolutely solid recall command that your Aussie will always come to before ever introducing him to other animals off-lead. If he begins to chase the livestock, call him to you and reward him for not chasing the animals.

While some Aussies are naturals at herding, it is always best to take some lessons or tips from a seasoned stock dog trainer early on if you want to herd livestock. For many, it can take several months of training to shape their instinct in such a way as to make it work for you!

Introducing your Aussie to animals like cats or pocket pets that don't live in your home is not really necessary. Most of these animals do not relish contact with dogs, and they are not something that your Aussie will likely see on a day to day basis outside of your home. Pocket pets especially are very fragile and could be accidentally harmed, so physical interactions between them and your Aussie are not recommended.

Greeting New People

Learning how to interact with other human beings is one of the most important skills your Aussie will ever acquire. People will be an inevitable and unavoidable part of their life. Many Aussies are reserved with new people, and this is entirely acceptable. However, they will still need to be able to tolerate people without fear.

Never allow someone to force themselves on your puppy if they are afraid; this will only deepen their fear. If your Aussie is intimidated, speak up and politely but firmly ask the person to give them space! It is your responsibility to protect your Aussie from a bad situation. If your Aussie is unsure, allow the person to calmly offer them a treat. After that, they should ignore your Aussie until they relax and solicit attention.

Some puppies are social butterflies. If this is the case, they can often become overly excited. Many people become excited when they see a puppy as well, which can further exacerbate the situation. Ask those greeting your puppy to speak calmly. Manners should always be enforced – your puppy should never be allowed to jump on or mouth people. This rule has to be absolute. Visitors often say they don't mind - but remind them that you do! They should not pet the puppy or pay attention to him until he can keep all four feet on the floor!

Expose your puppy to greetings with all sorts of people – tall, short, men, women, young, old, people in wheelchairs and wearing hats or sunglasses. Keep a calm and nonchalant attitude. If you are anxious or exuberant, your Aussie will reflect that attitude!

Photo Courtesy of
Lauren Kilby

Australian Shepherds and Children

Most Aussies are fiercely loyal to "their kids". However, strange children can be very intimidating to a dog. Young children are at eye level with your Aussie and can tend to unintentionally stare him down. Most are boisterous, with sudden movements and high-pitched voices. Puppies should be exposed to children often, and early on, so that they become used to their behavior. The same rule should apply to puppies with children as to adults – misbehavior should not be reinforced by allowing the puppy to jump on, chase, and nip children. If this occurs, calmly but firmly say, "No!" and redirect the puppy to an acceptable behavior, like a sit or down position. If he becomes too wound up, separate the puppy from the child and try again when he has calmed down.

Respect for dogs and their space should always be enforced with children. This is extremely important for the safety of the child and the comfort of the dog. Screaming, pulling hair or ears, slapping, grabbing the dog's face, grabbing at, and sitting on the dog are unacceptable. Most dogs are also uncomfortable with kisses and hugs. Warning signs that your Aussie is very uncomfortable with the situation are licking lips, yawning, squinting, turning the head away, the whites of the eyes showing, and attempting to get away from the situation. You must respect your dog and remove him from the situation immediately if you see these warning signs. These actions often precede a bite, and it is your responsibility to prevent this from happening! Many people claim they never saw a bite coming, but the reality is that the dog was giving warning signs all along – the human just didn't see them!

Take time to teach children, whether yours or someone else's, how to respect a dog. Children should always ask to pet your dog before approaching them. If they are given permission, they should be instructed to pet the dog calmly and gently on the back or the chest so that it is less intimidating. They should be calm and speak softly to the dog. Not only are you protecting your dog, but you are also teaching the child important life lessons. Dogs are a big part of our lives, and there is nothing more tragic than a bite occurring that could have been prevented. Kids and dogs can have wonderful relationships and share close bonds - if they are started off on the right foot and learn to respect one another!

When a pattern has been set that new experiences mean good things, this will be the foundation your Aussie will draw from for the rest of their life. A happy, well-adjusted dog that you can take anywhere with you without being afraid of how he may react is a precious thing indeed. Good, extensive, proper socialization will set your Aussie up for success! He will be all the happier for it, too, because he will approach life with confidence and be glad to spend more time with you!

Photo Courtesy of
Karie King
Kicking K Australian Shepehrds

CHAPTER 7
Physical and Mental Exercise

Many behavioral problems are caused by excess energy and boredom. Therefore, physical exercise and mental stimulation are key to a fit, happy Aussie. Australian Shepherds were bred to be highly intelligent working dogs who put in long hours on the ranch or farm. They need a job to do in order to be happy. There are many tasks and behaviors that can satisfy that need – and they don't have to include herding livestock!

Photo Courtesy of
Ryan Albanese

Age Appropriate Exercise

Physical exercise is an absolute necessity for dogs, just as in humans. However, puppies grow very rapidly, and the growth plates in their skeletons are prone to injuries that can cause permanent damage and chronic pain later in life. Because of this, short bursts of vigorous exercise on soft, stable surfaces is ideal. An easy rule to follow is five minutes of exercise per month of age up to twice per day; so if your puppy is four months old, he can exercise for up to 20 minutes at a time. Playtime on grass, sand, snow, or rubber matting acts as a shock absorber and helps to protect your puppy's bones. Avoid exercising on pavement, concrete, or slippery floors. Puppies should also never be asked to do repetitive jumping until they are at least 12 months old, as this too can cause irreversible damage. Normal jumping while frolicking during play is acceptable, but asking your puppy to repeatedly jump an obstacle can harm him.

HELPFUL TIP
Keeping Your Aussie Busy

Since Australian Shepherds were bred to work in the fields, herding sheep all day long, they have nearly infinite energy levels and quickly become bored and destructive. Luckily, we live in a time with many products available to keep your Aussie busy. Look for food-puzzle toys, treat-dispensing balls, and automatic ball-throwing machines to help keep your Aussie entertained and active.

Photo Courtesy of
Jennifer Rose

Types of Physical Exercise

The traditional walk is nearly always what first comes to mind when someone thinks about exercising their dog. Walking, jogging and biking with your Aussie is a great way to build endurance. While leash exercising your Aussie, always reinforce good leash manners at the same time. No one likes to be dragged by their dog! If your Aussie tries to pull, simply stop in your tracks and wait for him to turn toward you. Praise him when he does, then continue forward. If stopping doesn't get his attention, start backing up in the opposite direction he is pulling you. This is often enough to get him to turn his attention back towards the silly human that is going the wrong way! This rule should be enforced from the very first time you take your Aussie for a walk, and every time thereafter. Each time you allow yourself to be pulled, that behavior is being reinforced! The earlier you enforce this rule, the better. Ensure your Aussie wears a correctly fitted collar – you should be able to snugly fit two fingers under the collar, and no more.

When walking your Aussie on asphalt in warm weather, take care to ensure it isn't dangerously hot. An 86 degree day can have a pavement temperature of 135 degrees, which can burn paw pads. Check the safety of pavement temperature by placing the back of your hand on the asphalt; if you can't hold it there comfortably after 5 seconds, it's too hot for a walk.

Beware of walking great distances or spending extended periods outdoors in extreme temperatures. Hot weather can cause heat stroke; and cold temperatures, frost bite. Excessive panting and drooling, reddened gums, and damp, sweating skin are signs your Aussie needs to cool off as soon as possible. Move him to a shady area, dampen his body with cool water, and offer him cool water to drink. Avoid ice cold water, as cooling too rapidly can cause other complications. In cold weather, watch your Aussie carefully for signs preceding frostbite. Holding up his feet or shivering means he's too cold, and should be brought in to warm up immediately. Warming should be done slowly by offering warm water and wrapping your dog in warm, dry towels.

STORY

Hyper Hank

Australian Shepherd Hyper Hank and his owner Eldon McIntire became a famous team of Frisbee experts in the 1970s, even performing at the White House and at Super Bowl XII's preshow.

Treadmills can be a great tool to exercise your Aussie if you are short on time. Human treadmills can be used for walking, although dog-specific tread-

Photo Courtesy of
Mikayla McDonald

mills are ideal. You can introduce your Aussie to a treadmill by calling him onto it when it isn't running, and praising and rewarding him. Next, while he is not on the treadmill, turn it on to the slowest setting. Call your Aussie back to the treadmill, and reward him when he gets on or makes an attempt to do so. This can take time and may require some patience with some dogs, but in the end many learn to love working on a treadmill. Always supervise your Aussie when they are using the treadmill.

Another highly enjoyable form of exercise is to have your Aussie chase and retrieve balls or other toys. These short bursts of intense exercise are ideal for burning energy. Choose toys that are large enough that they can't accidentally become lodged in the airway. To teach your dog to bring the toy back to you, start by tossing the toy a short distance and rewarding him when he picks up the toy and brings it toward you. This can either be a food reward, or could be you throwing a second toy!

You can also incorporate games of fetch with swimming – while they are not inherently considered a water-loving breed, most Aussies enjoy swimming and it makes for great exercise as well. Be sure to avoid times of the year that are flooding and any bodies of deep, fast-moving water. Dogs are strong swimmers but even they can drown or be swept away by rough currents. Avoid stagnant bodies of water like late-summer ponds. If your Aussie does swim in stagnant water, you should bathe and thoroughly dry him afterwards. Not only will his coat likely smell rank, but the bacteria often found there can cause skin irritation or infections.

Many people use dog parks to exercise their Aussies. While playtime with other canine friends can be a fantastic way to burn off energy, be aware that many accidents and dog fights can occur at dog parks. Getting together a group of strange dogs can be risky. If you choose to visit a dog park, be absolutely sure you know how to read canine body language, closely monitor animal interactions, and always be prepared to intervene if things go sour. A dog avoiding the others by cowering or hiding, hard stares, whale eyes (the whites of the eyes showing), standing stiffly, curled lips, raised hackles, and low growls are all warning signs that trouble is imminent. Relaxed body postures, circular or wide-swinging tail wagging, and play bows are all good signs that everyone is getting along well.

Importance Of Mental Exercise

"The Aussie is very easily trained as they are inherently bred to work with their human partner. They are biddable and willing to please. They also have a keen sense of fairness. What this means is the owner should not expect the Aussie to be happy in an unrewarding and unnatural environment."

Tina Beck
Goldcrest Aussies

Photo Courtesy of Erick Heise

Photo Courtesy of
Karie King
Kicking K Australian Shepehrds

Australian Shepherds are an extremely intelligent breed. As such, they crave mental stimulation. Behavioral issues like digging, chewing household items, excessive barking, pacing, being unable to settle down, and chewing their own hair and paws can all be signs that your dog is not getting enough mental exercise. Mental stimulation is especially critical for puppies, as their brains are busy developing and learning. Giving older dogs regular brain workouts can keep them sharp longer, too.

Interestingly, mental exercise can actually tire your Aussie out physically! While not a substitute for necessary regular physical exercise, brain games and training can be a great way to give your dog an outlet on a rainy day if you'd rather not go outdoors for very long. Spending time with your dog and playing games to keep his brain active is a great bonding experience.

Photo Courtesy of
Jessica Graf

Tips For Keeping Your Australian Shepherd Occupied

There are many different ways you can challenge your Aussie's brain. Training can be very healthy and enjoyable for you and your dog. This includes teaching tricks, obedience commands, or training for dog sports like agility obstacle courses. Training should be kept upbeat, positive, and brief. A few short sessions of 5-10 minutes spread over a day is more fun and effective than one 20 minute session, especially for puppies with shorter attention spans.

There are many puzzle toys on the market for dogs today. Most of them entail making a dog think and work a little harder for a meal or treat, like toys or balls that can be stuffed with kibble or paste. You can also hide kibble or favorite toys around a room or yard and teach your dog to find them, or even to find you in a game of hide and seek. Alternatively, training your dog how to do scent work is also mentally challenging and rewarding. This involves teaching your Aussie to recognize to a specific odor, then hiding the scent in a room or in your yard and rewarding them when they correctly locate the scent.

Aussies love to feel like they are "helping out". If you don't have livestock for them to herd, you can find other jobs for them around the home. Teaching them to pick up dropped items for you, pick up their own toys and put them away in a box, or even to pull a sled or cart are just a few ideas that can make them feel useful.

CHAPTER 8
Training Your Australian Shepherd

"This is a very intelligent breed with a strong desire to learn"

Adriana Plum
Turkey Run Australian Shepherds

Photo Courtesy of
Lauren Dunning

"Aussies are very easy to train. The main word of advice is consistency. This goes for any type of training with an Aussie. If you are not consistent, they will remember and try to push to get their way."

Heidi Mobley
Western Hills Australian Shepherds

Training is something you will be doing with your Aussie - deliberately or not! Due to the breed's keen intelligence, the dogs are constantly learning and taking cues from you. As a result, it pays to spend time actively training your Aussie and reinforcing the behaviors you want to see. Good training methods take into account your dog's point of view and makes things clear to him. Take the reins and be proactive, teach your Aussie what you expect of him in the beginning rather than waiting until there is a problem to address!

Benefits of Proper Training

Everyone loves a well-mannered dog. What many new dog owners fail to realize is that achieving good behavior often takes a lot of time and effort – it's work! It does not magically happen overnight. That said, training absolutely can and should be a fun activity for both you and your dog. It's one of the best ways to bond with your Aussie and is an investment in your future together.

Photo Courtesy of
Cynthia Hokes

Clear Expectations

"They are super easy to train IF you establish your authority. If you are over-ly easy on them or aren't perceived as the boss, they will take that job for you!"

Joanne Harvell
Canyon Lake Aussies

One of the keys to effective training is having clear expectations and goals in mind, and breaking those expectations down into pieces and steps that your Aussie can understand. You can't train your dog once per month and expect to make progress. You also won't make progress overnight if you have a problem behavior that has been unintentionally reinforced for some time. Expect to set aside a 5-10 minute session time at least several times per week, preferably daily. Look for opportunities to incorporate training into your everyday activities as well. Mealtimes, walks, and playtimes can all be used to creatively reinforce behaviors you are teaching your Aussie.

Consistency is key to communicating clear expectations to your Aussie. If he is allowed to pull on the leash some of the time, he will not understand when it is ok or when it is not, and will try to pull every single time. If you allow him to drag you along, you are reinforcing that behavior because you are continuing to move with him in the direction he wants to go. If instead you do not ever allow your dog to pull on the leash by stopping in your tracks and waiting for the leash tension to slacken before continuing forward, he will quickly learn that it is not acceptable, it does not work, and consequently he will rarely pull.

Everyone who interacts with your Aussie – family, friends, and visitors - also need to understand your expectations. If jumping up on you is not ok, it isn't ok for other people to allow that behavior either. If your visitors react positively to your Aussie jumping on them by petting and rewarding him with attention, your dog will likely also try it with you to see if it works again - even if you've previously established that it is not. Situations like this can rapidly undermine your training efforts!

STORY
Rodeo and Movie Stars

Since Australian Shepherds are so trainable, they quickly became associated with the rodeo after World War I. Jay Sisler had a show with his Aussies Stubby, Shorty, and Queenie that was so popular that Disney made two movies about them!

Photo Courtesy of
Mary Sanders

Operant Conditioning Basics

"In general, Aussies are super smart. But, as with any breed, they must be taught to think. Shaping or operant conditioning using clicker training seems to work really well. Most Aussies are very food driven and the food drive can be used as a reward for correct responses to training."

Joan Fry
Bella Loma Kennels

Operant conditioning is a method of training that uses rewards and consequences to affect behavior. Operant conditioning actually happens every time you interact with your dog, and every time he interacts with the world around him, as positive and negative consequences naturally occur. Essentially, associations are made between a behavior and a consequence. For example, as a child if you touched a hot stove burner, you experienced pain as a negative consequence. You then associated pain with a hot burner, and thereafter probably avoided touching that surface. You also made positive associations, like if you completed a chore and were rewarded with a treat by your parents. Dogs learn similarly, but things that we perceive as positive or negative are not always viewed the same way by our dogs! If your dog jumps up on you, you may consider pushing him off you or scolding him to be a negative consequence. However, the opposite is often true – you are touching your dog and speaking to him, both of which are often viewed positively by the dog in this situation.

Positive Reinforcements

Positive reinforcement can come in many forms. The most common rewards are food, toys, verbal praise, and physical affection like petting. Often, a dog will work harder for one or two types of reward than the others; for some, food has the highest immediate value, while for others, a favorite toy beats all. Positive reinforcements can also come in the form of a favorable outcome to the dog. For example, if you want to teach your dog not to race out the door ahead of you, simply don't allow him to exit the door until he is sitting calmly and you have given your permission. In this case, the reward is being allowed to move through the doorway. Many dogs can be trained almost entirely using positive reinforcement methods.

"Aussies love to please their humans and have fantastic focus! You will be amazed at how quickly they learn. And the more you teach, the easier it is for them to learn. Being a sensitive breed, they respond well to positive reinforcement training. Harsh methods can cause an Aussie to shut down and appear as if they are stubborn, but, in actuality, they only want to please."

Gayle Silberhorn
Big Run Aussies

Negative Reinforcements

Negative reinforcement can include punitive forms such as verbal reprimands, various correction collars, and physical correction. It can also simply take the form of negative consequences. Revisiting the doorway example – being blocked from exiting, such as closing the door, is a negative consequence to the dog. This is often the most gentle form of negative reinforcement, and can have great results when executed properly. Striking, yelling at, or physically dominating your dog are never acceptable forms of correction! Proper physical correction can include things like a quick firm tug on the leash to return your dog to heel position, or gently placing a dog into a position like a sit or down. Appropriate verbal reprimands should be used only to draw attention to the behavior as something undesirable – a simple, but firm "ack!" is all that is needed.

The Dangers of Punishment-Based Training

"Aussie puppies can be vocal, get the 'zoomies', and go over the top with their enthusiasm. Engagement should be rewarded and punishment used very sparingly. They are thinkers, teach them to think."

Joan Fry
Bella Loma Kennels

Most dogs, and Aussies in particular, do not thrive under a punitive-based training method. While you should never have to bribe your dog for everything, it is difficult to learn in an environment where you constantly fear punishment. Dogs generally do not do things to deliberately frustrate or disappoint us – they just think like dogs, not human beings. The vast majority of the time, we really have only ourselves to blame for our dog's failures.

Punishment-based training often causes dogs to become unwilling, un-enthusiastic workers. Instead of a happy can-do attitude, they offer only what they must to avoid punishment. They may want to avoid you instead of spend time with you. In effect, this type of correction is damaging to your relationship. Oftentimes, you can see rapid short-term results with a punishment-based method, only to see the behavior reoccur within weeks or months or a new undesirable behavior crop up to take its place. Instead of being fun, training becomes a source of fear and stress for your dog. If you were punished in school for every wrong answer and rarely praised for correct answers, would you enjoy learning there? Probably not...and you'd likely resent the teacher, too!

Hiring a Trainer and Attending Classes

While you can and should be training your Aussie regularly at home, it is often extremely valuable to have someone experienced give you guidance and insight. Many times, we do things that impede our dogs' success without even realizing it. A professional can often pinpoint the problem by simply watching you interact with your dog. The most important thing for you to realize is that classes and professional trainers are not going to train your dog for you – they are going to teach you how to train your own dog. A trainer can start a little of the work for you during a session, but really it is up to you to follow through at home if you truly want your dog to be successful.

Veterinarians, groomers, and dog clubs can often recom-

Photo Courtesy of Amanda Watkins

mend trainers in your area. When choosing a trainer, select one who primarily uses positive reinforcement training. Ask if you can observe a class, and see if the trainer stays positive and upbeat. Good trainers that work with owners need to have patience with the dogs, and also with people! Do they explain their methods in a way you understand? Is the dog responding positively during the training session?

Whether attending a class or hiring a professional for private lessons, make sure you do your homework. If you want to make progress and get the most out of a session, practice the things you learned at home during the week. Becoming a good dog trainer takes time, even just for manners and basic obedience, and often requires people to change their behavior and the way they interact with their dogs.

Having Fun In Performance Sports

"Dog sports and socialization classes are a better place for exercise of the body and mind then 'dog parks'. Treat dog parks as accidents waiting to happen."

Francine Guerra
Alias Aussies

Australian Shepherds are well-known in the world of dog sports as a force to be reckoned with. With their enthusiasm, intelligence, and agility they can often excel at almost anything. Training your dog for competition will deepen your bond as you both learn how to play in your chosen sport. There are many different things you can compete in with your dog, from timed obstacle courses to herding livestock in an arena. Most of these events require a great amount of teamwork. If you are interested in competing in a sport with your Aussie, contact your local dog club to see if there are classes or mentors available to help you get started. Here are just some of the sports you can participate in with your Aussie:

Agility
You must direct your dog through a timed obstacle course. Jumps, tunnels, teeter-totters, and climbing an A-frame are just some of the obstacles you might see in this fast-paced sport.

*Photo Courtesy of
Cynamon Rei Moseley*

Obedience

Competitive obedience includes heeling, recalls, and stays in the lower levels. At higher levels of competition your dog may be required to jump as directed, distinguish and retrieve articles with your scent on them, and more.

Rally-Obedience

This relatively new sport combines heeling, obedience commands, and various maneuvers on a course directed with signs.

Herding

You must direct your dog to move livestock around a course of chutes and gates. Sheep, cattle, and ducks are the most common types of livestock used.

Nosework or Scent Work

Your dog must be trained to identify certain scents hidden in various items or places, either in a room or a set area outdoors.

Photo Courtesy of Lisa Ricard

Tracking

In this sport, your dog must be able to follow a scent trail and lead you to where the trail ends.

Flyball

This is a very fast team sport – four dogs take turns in a relay over a line of hurdles, catch a ball released from a box, and race back with the ball to their team.

Dock Diving

Your dog must leap off a dock into a pool as far as they can.

If you are interested in pursuing a sport with your Aussie, contact your local kennel club and see what classes they offer. You can also search the American Kennel Club or Australian Shepherd Club Of America event calendars on their websites. Find an event near you to attend, and get connected with those in the sport who can help direct you to regional clubs and associations.

HELPFUL TIP
Dog Sports

There is not a one-size-fits-all training method. Just like people, dogs are individuals. As a whole, if your Aussie is responding to your chosen method with enthusiasm, then it's working. If it isn't working, don't be afraid to try something new, or to get experienced help. Training should be fun, whether for basic manners or for a dog sport!

Since Australian Shepherds are so active and intelligent, they often thrive in dog sports like agility and flyball. If those don't interest you, teaching your Aussie lots of new tricks on a regular basis will help keep his brain engaged and working hard.

CHAPTER 9
Basic Obedience Commands

"They can be a bit controlling in active situations. I call them fun po-lice. Having a good bond with your dog with obedience and manners will help. A good down stay, leave it, or enough command is a must to have. Both behaviors are instinct, so having an outlet like learning Treibball (herding a large ball around the yard) may help, or even just a fun sport class. Some Aussies will get frustrated if they don't have an outlet and start barking excessively."

Melonie Eso
WCK Aussies

Photo Courtesy of
Hope Bailey

Obedience training should not be considered optional – it is an essential part of your responsibility to your Australian Shepherd. While dogs have been bred for thousands of years to become a part of man's world and to perform tasks to better our lives, they do not come pre-programmed knowing what we expect of them. It is our job to teach dogs what humans' expectations are, in a way that they can understand! Basic obedience training is the first step in that journey.

Tips for Successful Training

There is not a one-size-fits-all method of teaching a command or addressing a problem behavior. What works for one dog, may not work for another. In this chapter we will go over the most common methods of teaching seven basic commands or behaviors.

Most dogs pick up physical cues, like hand signals, faster than verbal cues. This makes sense from a dog's perspective, as they communicate with each other primarily through body language. Our voices can change significantly depending on our emotions in a given moment, but a simple gesture of our hand is usually fairly consistent. Dogs are extremely perceptive to subtle cues and changes, so be aware of your body language and tone of voice when working with your Aussie. An excited command may mean something different than one given in a calm or frustrated voice, unless your dog has been taught that they are the same. If you teach a dog to sit with a hand signal and always use your right hand, he will need to be taught that the same signal given with the left hand means sit, too!

When you are teaching a verbal command, wait to use your word for the behavior ("sit", "down", etc) until the dog is beginning to really understand the behavior. Make sure you have your dog's attention before giving a command, and only ever give one command at a time. If you say "sit, sit, sit!", and after the third time you say it, your dog sits and is rewarded for it, he will believe that "sit, sit, sit!" is the command, not just one "sit"!

Understand that most dogs do not generalize well. They may learn to sit consistently on command in your kitchen, but as soon as you take them to another room or outside, they must be taught that "sit" in the kitchen is the same everywhere else. Practice in different places – different rooms in your home, the front yard, the back yard, at the park and in dog-friendly stores. It is also easier to first teach new commands in an area with fewer distractions (like at home), then increase the distractions (training out in public) as your dog grasps the command.

Photo Courtesy of
Kayla Umbaugh

Be sure to keep sessions short – 5-10 minutes is usually plenty. Keep training positive and fun. Always end on a good note. If your Aussie is struggling with something, ask him for a behavior they can succeed at, and then end the session there. After a training session, a short break of five minutes in a crate often helps dogs further process what they have just learned.

Behavior Marking And Release Words

Before you begin teaching obedience commands, you will need to have a way to communicate to your Aussie that he has done something correctly. This is called a behavior marker. You will also need to teach a release word – this tells your Aussie that he may leave a position (like sit, down, and so on).

Behavior markers are a way to tell your dog "that was correct; a reward is coming!" It can be a word, like "Yes!" or "Good!", as long as it is always the same. Markers can also be a tool called a clicker, that makes a single clicking sound when you press a button. The benefit of a clicker is that it always sounds exactly the same, whereas your voice can change depending on your emotions. However, either method will provide satisfactory results, and you can use both.

Before using a behavior marker, you must "charge" it – that is to say, you must assign meaning to it for your dog to give it its power. Initially, your Aussie won't understand that a click or a "yes" means anything. To charge a marker, have a handful of small, preferably soft high-value treats that your Aussie really likes. Low fat string cheese or soft commercial training treats are good. Have your dog come to you. Use your marker, pause for just a moment, then give a treat as a reward. Repeat this 10 times. It should be: yes/click, pause, reward, pause; yes/click, pause, reward, pause. End the session and repeat the next day. By then, your Aussie will probably have figured out that the marker means good things are coming!

Using a behavior marker requires excellent timing. You must use your marker at the ex-

HELPFUL TIP
The Importance of "Drop It" and "Leave It"

Since Australian Shepherds can get into trouble trying to keep themselves entertained, teaching your Aussie to "drop it" could save his life if he snags something inedible, thinking it will make a great snack. Meanwhile, "leave it" may prevent him from taking a dust bath in a pile of horse manure.

act moment your Aussie performs the behavior you want. If you ask your dog to sit, you will want to mark the behavior as soon as his bottom touches the floor. The better you are at correct timing, the faster your dog will learn a behavior.

Release words are important because they teach the dog that he must remain in a position until you tell him otherwise. This is a foundation for stays. Rather than thinking of "sit" and "stay" as two separate commands, it makes more sense from the dog's perspective if when you teach "sit," he learns he must stay sitting until you release him. Common words used for release are "okay", "break", or "free". Choose one, and always remember when you give your dog a position command like sit or stay, that you are the one who must release him. If he moves before you release him, correct him gently by placing him back into the position. Be sure to release him before he does so himself and reward him with some affection or praise afterward. As a general rule, you should not give treats after a release, as the release itself is the main reward.

Basic Commands

Sit

To teach "sit," first get your dog's attention. Hold a small treat between your fingers and allow your dog to smell what you have. Now raise the treat slowly up over his nose and head. Your dog's nose should tilt up and back

Photo Courtesy of
Colleen Bradley

to follow the lure. As this happens, his bottom tends to go down. As soon as his bottom touches the floor, immediately use your marker and reward! Repeat this several more times before taking a break. If your dog has a tendency to back up instead of sit, try moving the lure higher and more slowly. You can also try this against a wall or in a corner to stop your Aussie from backing up. Once your dog is starting to grasp what you're asking, you can add the verbal command (i.e. "sit") and start "fading the lure". Fading the lure is when you begin to ask for the behavior without using the food to lure the dog into position. Use food every other time, every third or fourth time, then eliminate it completely. By this point, you should be able to simply raise your hand palm up to signal him to sit. You should now also make sure to use your release word before the dog gets up. He should only be expected to stay sitting for a few seconds at this point.

STORY
Guinness World Record

Australian Shepherd/Border Collie mix Sweet Pea holds a Guinness World Record for walking 328 feet with a soda can balanced on his head for just under three minutes.

Lie Down

To teach your dog to lie down, first get your dog's attention and tell him to sit. Take a small treat between your fingers, hold it in front of his nose and allow your dog to smell what you have. Now lower your hand straight down towards the floor. Your dog should begin to crouch to follow the lure. As this happens, immediately use your marker and reward! Your dog does not have to go down all the way to the floor at first. Repeat this several more times, each time dropping your hand closer to the floor. If your dog tends to want to stand up, you may be luring with your hand too far in front of the dog or dropping your hand too quickly. Once your dog is starting to grasp what you are asking, you can add the verbal command "down" and start fading the lure. Eventually, you should be able to lower your hand toward the floor to signal him to lie down. Remember, once he understands what the command to lie down means, you need to be the one to release him.

Stay

By this point, your dog should have a good grasp of the sit and lie down commands. You also will have already laid the foundation for a solid "stay" command by incorporating a release word. Now, you are going to begin increasing the amount of time before releases. Ask your dog to sit. Wait three seconds, use your marker, reward, and release. Repeat this a few times in a sit, and again in a lie down. Each session, increase

Photo Courtesy of Kilby

the amount of time by 3-5 seconds. If he gets up before you release him, place him back into the position and reduce the amount of time by a few seconds. When he has mastered staying in position with you standing still in front of him, you can add a "stay" verbal command and begin adding distractions. Try taking a step to the side or moving your arms at first and rewarding him if he stays. Increase the difficulty a little each session. Go back a step if your dog seems to be struggling. Eventually, you should be able to walk all the way around him, walk twenty feet away, and do jumping jacks while he stays. This takes time and creative persistence. Each new distraction is a new challenge for your dog.

Come

To teach your dog to reliably come when he is called, you must make this command the most wonderful thing in the world to your dog. Start by calling your dog's name and a command like "come" or "here" when you are in the house. Use your marker and reward heartily with happy praise and a food reward when he comes to you. Throw a little party! When he is reliably coming to you in the house, take him outside and work on a 20′ long line or in a safely fenced area. When he gets a distance away from you, call his name and your command to come. Verbally praise him when he comes

Photo Courtesy of Sheila Romanski

toward you and reward him enthusiastically when he reaches you. Never, ever, punish or scold your dog when he comes to you. All this teaches your dog is that coming to you means that he will be punished, and therefore he will instead, avoid you. If you need to call your dog to you to do something unpleasant, like a bath, be sure to take a moment to reward him before putting him in the tub! Always reward your dog for coming to you, no matter how frustrated you may be. Teaching your dog to reliably come is important for their safety; it could save their life if they were to get loose or be in a life-threatening situation.

Give/Drop

Think of this command like a trade. You want your dog to willingly offer up whatever he has in the belief that you will give him something better in exchange. To teach your dog to "give" or "drop it", with treats in hand call your dog to you and offer a toy, or wait until he is playing with you by himself. Then show your dog the treat, and as soon as he drops the toy use your marker and reward him with the treat. Give the toy back and repeat this a few more times. If your dog loses interest in the toy that's okay, just end the session there. If you find your dog is more interested in the toy than your treats, try using a lower value item or try some different treats. You want the food to be more important than the toy! When your dog readily drops the toy at the offer of a treat, try keeping the treats in your hand behind your back and reaching for the toy with the other hand. If your dog doesn't drop it, offer the food again and repeat the first step a few more times. Eventually, start practicing this with higher value items, like safe edible dog chews or higher value toys. Teaching your dog to drop items on command is very important in the event they are chewing on something unsafe or toxic.

Walking on a Leash

Teaching your dog to walk politely on a leash takes time and consistency. The earlier you establish the ground rules, the less problems you will have in the long run. Firstly, your dog has to learn that pulling you gets them nowhere. Never ever let your dog pull you. Ever. If your dog starts to pull you, just stop dead in your tracks. Usually that is enough to make him stop and turn to look at you to see why you stopped. When he turns to look at you, use your marker and reward. Try stepping forward again, and reward when he stays with you for a few steps, then five to six steps. You can use verbal praise at any time but try to space out the food rewards so that the dog does not become dependent on them. If you have a dog that continues to pull even when you stop and stand your ground, start to back up. Keep backing up until he looks at you, then use your marker and reward. Be sure to praise and reward your Aussie when he stays close enough to you to have a slack leash for several steps. Remember, dogs thrive on consistency. If you let them get away with leash pulling one time, they will do it the next time and your hard work can quickly be undone. Even seasoned dogs need occasional leash manners reminders!

Training takes time and perseverance, but the reward of having an Aussie that fully understands what is expected of him will make life better both for you and your dog. Australian Shepherds live to please the humans they love, and there is nothing they won't do for you!

CHAPTER 10
Dealing with Unwanted Behaviors

Misbehavior in dogs is caused by several factors – developmental stages in puppies, boredom or excess energy, inherent temperament problems, and unclear or ambiguous expectations on our part. Dogs do not intentionally do things to frustrate or disappoint humans. Unfortunately, many people misunderstand their dog and apply human thoughts and feelings, which often does the dogs we love a disservice. Remember, your dog is not a human in a fur coat – he is a domesticated carnivore living in a human world. He is highly adapted to living by your side, but he is still a dog. Oftentimes, we need to stop and consider the world from our dog's point of view.

Photo Courtesy of
Joshua Martin

What is Bad Behavior in Dogs?

Common problems Australian Shepherds face include chewing household items and other destructive shenanigans, including barking, jumping on people or furniture, and nipping at heels. However, consider again that your Aussie is not trying to be disobedient or disappoint you. It's likely that either his needs are not being met, or you have not established what is and is not acceptable behavior for him.

Preventing Problem Behaviors

"Most Aussies want a job in order to keep them happy. They look for ways to help and will create jobs if you don't give them one."

Allison Lutterman
DreamWinds

Prevention is key to having as few behavioral problems to address as possible. This often starts at the very beginning when selecting a puppy to bring home – considering individual temperament and the way puppies are raised by their breeder has an enormous lifelong impact on your Aussie. Overly shy, anxious, or aggressive parent dogs often produce offspring with the same problems they themselves have. These ingrained temperamental flaws can often foreshadow a myriad of other difficulties in later life, and while most can be mitigated to a degree, it is often challenging and time consuming at best.

After you've brought your Aussie home, setting a foundation of clear expectations is key. Take an all-or-nothing approach. Consider what you have done to feed into these behaviors. Many times, we ourselves are causing or encouraging the very behaviors we find offensive! Understand, too, that puppies and even adult dogs new to your household are still learning the rules. They will make mistakes, and that is normal. Puppies es-

HELPFUL TIP
Causes of Unwanted Behaviors

Australian Shepherds rarely develop behavioral problems out of the blue. Common causes of unwanted behaviors include:
• Boredom
• Not enough exercise
• Separation anxiety
• Lack of training
• Poor socialization as a puppy

pecially are blank slates, and they go through developmental stages where they can seem to forget the rules for a time. Patience, repetition, and consistency will see you both through these phases.

The third key to prevention is ensuring that your Aussie's physical and mental needs are being met. When they do not get enough physical or mental exercise, this will often manifest itself through excessively destructive or compulsive behaviors. Ensure they are getting enough exercise each day, and spend time training and playing with them!

"Aussies need to RUN! Not just a casual walk around the block, but full out run. I can't emphasize that enough. They are working dogs that need to exercise their body and mind. Brain games can help when the weather does not cooperate. Puzzles, tricks and training are all good. Be determined to exercise this breed every day, or you will have a stressed, destructive dog on your hands."

Gayle Silberhorn
Big Run Aussies

Fixing Bad Habits

Chewing

A dog's need to chew is completely natural – this strengthens his jaw and helps keep his teeth clean. Puppies especially, are prone to chew more due to teething, just like human babies. The first step towards solving inappropriate chewing is acknowledging that natural desire by providing a variety of toys that are safe, well-made and intended for your Aussie. These should always be available to your dog. Next, you should try to keep temptation out of reach, especially for young puppies. Pick up shoes, children's toys, and other items your Aussie may want to snag. Keep your Aussie in his crate with a few toys when you cannot be around to monitor him. If he does manage to get ahold of something inappropriate, calmly but firmly say "No!" or "Ah ah!". Remove the object and offer one of his own toys instead. When he takes it, be sure to praise him.

If your Aussie is determined to chew on an inappropriate object or piece of furniture, try using a bitter apple chew deterrent spray on the item. The vile flavor quickly discourages this behavior and can help break the habit by creating a negative association with the item.

Digging

This behavior can stem from boredom, escape attempts, pursuing prey like moles, be a way to stay cool, or due to a desire to save toys and treats for later. Digging does not pose a problem in and of itself to your dog but can cause considerable damage to your yard. Firstly, ensure your Aussie has plenty of toys and is getting enough exercise and mental stimulation. If the weather is warm, make certain there is plenty of cool shade or keep him in the house during the warmest parts of the day. If he really does just enjoy digging, consider having a designated sandbox for your Aussie in a shady area.

If you catch him digging in an inappropriate area, interrupt the behavior with a calm but firm "No!" and redirect him to his designated digging area or a suitable toy. Often once a hole has been started a dog will return to it, so discourage further digging in that area by placing rocks or chicken wire over it. Some dogs are discouraged when you place a few pieces of their own excrement in the bottom of a hole before filling it.

Separation Anxiety

The distress this issue can cause for dogs and the humans that love them can be significant. Separation anxiety happens when your dog experiences mild to severe distress when left alone, or when separated from a person or other dog in the home he is particularly attached to. Signs of separation anxiety can include pacing, barking and whining, drooling, panting, shaking, destructive behaviors like chewing or clawing at doors and windows, or eliminating in the house. It is important to be able to tell the difference between true separation anxiety or other behavioral issues – for example, accidents in the house could just signify the need for better potty training, not anxiety.

If your dog has mild to moderate separation anxiety, seriously consider crate training and spending time building a very positive association with the crate. Some dogs with mild anxiety feel more secure in their crates when left alone. Put your Aussie in his crate for short periods throughout the day and always include special treats or toys. Also, avoid only putting him in his crate when you intend to leave. You don't want your dog always associating the crate with a negative event like being left alone.

Make sure to exercise your dog thoroughly before leaving him for any length of time. If he is tired, he will have less energy for destructive behavior. Also, start breaking up the routine you follow before you leave home. If you usually put on your shoes, pick up your keys and then leave, instead

Photo Courtesy of Amanda Gabriel

put on your shoes and then go sit at the table for a few minutes. Make your routine a little different every day and be unpredictable. This will help prevent your Aussie's anxiety from building since he will no longer know which events precede your leaving. When you do finally leave, make sure to keep calm and avoid showing any emotion. Quietly put your dog in his safe space or kennel with a treat-stuffed toy or chew and simply walk away. Our emotion or attempts to console our dogs often just make matters worse and increases their anxiety.

Nipping and Mouthing

Mouthing and play biting is a natural part of puppies' play with each other; however, human skin tears far easier than a dog's! This behavior can become unsafe if not discouraged from the start. If your dog or puppy playfully mouths or nips you, say "No!" and abruptly stop paying any attention. Move away and don't look at, touch, or talk to him. After a few minutes, calmly re-engage the dog. Repeat this process if he tries to mouth you again. He will quickly learn that when he uses his mouth on you, all the fun stops.

If your Aussie likes to nip at heels, especially when a person or child is moving, first say "No!", and stop all motion. Ask him to perform a trick, or a task like a sit/stay to redirect his attention. Reward him when he complies. Especially determined heel nippers may require bitter apple chew deterrent spray on your pants at first to further discourage this behavior.

Jumping on People and Furniture

This is a problem behavior that people often unintentionally encourage. Allowing paws on furniture or people should be an all-or-nothing rule. You cannot discourage your Aussie one day from jumping on you to greet you but invite him up the next. This just confuses your dog and makes it difficult or impossible for him to understand your expectations. Everyone that encounters your Aussie needs to follow these rules as well. If it is not ok for your dog to jump on you, it shouldn't be ok to jump on other people either.

Remember to never reward your Aussie for jumping on you. Oftentimes people try to push dogs away or scold them. However, you are then touching them and paying attention to them - both of which your Aussie views as rewards. If he does jump on you, immediately turn your back. Do not look at, touch, or talk to him. When your Aussie has four paws on the floor, calmly praise him and try again to pet and greet him. You may have to repeat this several times, but he will soon learn (with occasional reminders) that four paws on the floor gets him the attention he craves. Practice this with another person and your Aussie on leash as well; have your assistant come up to greet your Aussie while you hold the leash. If your dog tries to jump on the person greeting him, the person should immediately back up out of reach. Once he has four paws on the floor again and the dog is calm, the assistant can try approaching again and reward him calmly with treats or praise and affection if the dog resists the temptation to jump up.

Allowing dogs on furniture or in bed is often a matter of personal preference. However, understand that it is easier to set boundaries in the beginning (and allow privileges later) than it is to undo a learned pattern of behavior down the road. If you decide that you would rather not have your

Aussie allowed on furniture, make a separate place for him – a cushy dog bed is a good choice. If he gets on the furniture, calmly but firmly say "No!" and call or lure him off. Take a favorite toy or a special chew and use it to direct him to his own space. Praise him when he settles down on his own furniture instead!

Inappropriate Behavior with Other Pets

Most often, this problem comes in the form of bullying other pets in the household. If your Aussie gets too rough during play and does things like body slamming, neck biting, or forcing the other dog onto it's back, it is time to intervene. Put a flat buckle collar on your Aussie and attach a lead at least 6 feet long before releasing him to play. When you see an inappropriate behavior, immediately say "No!" or "Ah-ah!" in a firm but calm tone of voice and take him by the leash to make the fun stop. It also helps to diffuse situations before they escalate – if you see your Aussie getting too riled, call him to you and reward him for obeying. Ask him to do a trick or sit/stay and reward before releasing him to play again. You can use these methods to stop your Aussie from chasing or playing roughly with cats and other pets, as well. Be sure to praise and reward him when he is playing nicely or interacting calmly with your other pets.

Growling and Barking

Dogs communicate primarily through body language and scent, however, vocalizations do play a part. Barking can happen during play, or act as an alert or warning. Most barking is excessive alert barking at a window or out in the yard. To control this, interrupt your dog with a firm "No!" and redirect him to a toy or ask him to perform a different behavior or trick instead. Reward and praise him when he complies.

Growling can happen during play, like during a game of tug; or, it can be a serious warning that precedes a bite and should always be taken seriously. Never punish your dog for growling, as this just teaches him not to give a warning and creates a very dangerous situation. Most often, your dog is uncomfortable or afraid and this is his way of telling whatever is causing his fear to back off. If your dog is growling at you or a family member, seek professional help.

When to Call a Professional

Potentially dangerous problem behaviors, like biting and aggression or extreme shyness, as well as any behavioral problems you have been working on for a period of weeks or months that have not seen any marked improvement, should always be evaluated by an animal behaviorist or professional trainer who specializes in these types of cases. Unfortunately, when you are in the midst of a severe problem it can be difficult to see where things are going wrong until you have an expert observing the situation from the outside.

A behaviorist will usually have a phone call or face-to-face interview with you and ask many questions about your dog and the problems you are facing. Then, they'll set up a meeting in person to try to witness the behavior and offer solutions tailored to your specific circumstances. Many times, what we may think is the cause is not the root issue at all. After your evaluation, the behaviorist will give you recommendations to work on at home and set up follow-up evaluations to ensure progress is being made.

The old saying "an ounce of prevention is worth a pound of cure" could not be truer when it comes to raising and training your Aussie. However, even the most prepared owners can and do run into problems from time to time, and that is ok! Learn to recognize problems early on, and work to correct them before they become a major issue. Never be ashamed to seek advice from a qualified professional; many severe behavioral problems could be avoided if only we asked for help when we first needed it.

CHAPTER 11

Traveling with Your Australian Shepherd

"They want to go everywhere you do."

Allison Lutterman
Dream Winds Australian Shepherds

Aussies are often called Velcro dogs, and no wonder – most want to be your constant shadow. They make great traveling companions and enjoy living it up on the road with their people. However, other times it is necessary for them to remain behind. In this chapter we will go over how to make traveling with your Aussie a safe, smooth ride - and alternatively, how best to keep him safe and comfortable when he cannot accompany you.

Photo Courtesy of Karyn Hynd

Dog Carriers and Car Restraints

"My Australian Shepherds are excellent travel companions. They enjoy car rides. Aussies are extremely adaptable as long as their human is involved. However, they should be secured by dog seat belts or crates."

Francine Guerra
Alias Aussies

Crates are always the safest place for your dog to ride in the car. They should be large enough for your dog to comfortably stand up and turn around in. Crates constructed from stronger materials like sheet aluminum or steel will offer better protection in the event of a crash than those made of fabric or plastic. The safest place for crates is on the floor or in the rear of the vehicle. Strapping crates down firmly can further prevent them from shifting or moving in an accident.

Dog seat belts are growing in popularity and can be a good alternative to a crate if your vehicle does not have room for the latter. They

Photo Courtesy of Megan Rogers

should be a harness style and fitted properly, with well-padded straps that are as broad as possible to distribute the force of impact. The tethers should be short and attach at the back of the harness, not the neck. Ideally, your dog should always be in the back seat of the vehicle. Deploying airbags or the failure of the harness in the front seat could severely injure or kill your Aussie.

Preparing for Travel

HELPFUL TIP
Flying with an Aussie

Australian Shepherds are too large to be allowed inside the cabin of an airplane (unless they're qualified service dogs), so they're forced to ride in cargo. While this is generally safe, plenty of accidents do happen every year, and it isn't fun for your dog even on a good day. Try taking your Aussie for a road trip, if possible, to avoid flying.

The amount of preparation needed for a trip with your Aussie will likely vary greatly depending on where you are headed and how long you will be gone. Before short trips and in general, make sure you give your Aussie time to relieve himself before hitting the road. Avoid feeding him a meal within a few hours of the trip, especially if he's prone to carsickness or is a puppy. Clear away any items or clutter if your dog won't be secured in a crate, and ensure nothing adjacent to a crate can be pulled through the sides and chewed.

Keeping identification on your Aussie when you're traveling is extremely important. Pets can get lost during travel, and they are far more difficult to recover in an unfamiliar location. The best option for all dogs, whether or not they travel frequently, is a microchip. This permanent form of identification, about the size of a grain of rice, is implanted under your Aussie's skin with a unique identification number. The number can then be registered into a national database. If your Aussie ever gets lost and picked up, animal control organizations and veterinarian clinics keep scanners that can read the ID number and trace it back to you. The second option, which can also be good for supplemental and quick identification, is a fitted flat buckle collar with your contact information written or embroidered onto it. Tags are often used but can get snagged and broken off. If you use tags, ensure they are securely attached.

When packing for a longer trip, make a list of things to bring. This includes food, bowls, any medications or supplements, a spare crate, bags for picking up waste, and toys. Always keep paper towels and bags for disposal on hand in your vehicle. You never need them until you don't have them! It's also wise to keep a copy of your Aussie's proof of rabies vaccination in case of an emergency, as most states require dogs to be vaccinated.

While most Aussies enjoy going for rides with their owners, some are fearful at first. With new puppies or dogs that are afraid, start introductions to the vehicle slowly. Start with the engine off and place your dog in the car for a minute or two. Reward him with treats and praise, then allow him to exit the vehicle. Build up the amount of time slowly and begin having the engine running or driving around the block before returning home. Your Aussie will soon associate car rides with fun, especially because he gets to be with you!

Flying and Hotel Stays

"Aussies make wonderful travel companions as long as they are trained. I personally would suggest taking a crate along if you are going to a hotel. This is great if you step out to get a bite of food, they will be comfortable and safe in their crate."

Heidi Mobley
Western Hills Australian Shepherds

Transporting your Aussie via plane presents its own set of challenges, but it can be done well with proper planning. Australian Shepherds are usually not small enough to be brought with you as carry-on baggage unless they are young puppies. Carry-on restrictions vary by airline and can be a good option if you are fetching a puppy home from a breeder. Most Aussies will be flown in a pressurized cargo area instead.

Before you plan to fly your Aussie, contact the airline you will be using and make note of their requirements. Once you've booked a flight, you will need to schedule a visit to the vet for a health certificate and prepare an airline-approved crate. Crates need to be hard sided (usually plastic) and large enough for the dog to stand up, turn around and lie down comfortably. They should be in good repair with firmly secured bolts. Food and water dishes should be securely attached to the inside of

Photo Courtesy of
Chris Weitzner

the kennel door, and a bag of kibble taped to the top of the crate. Shredded newspaper, towels, or an absorbent low sided bed will suffice to line it.

Arrive early at the airport and be sure to thoroughly exercise your Aussie and allow him plenty of time to relieve himself. Avoid feeding a large meal before the flight. Once he's on the plane, don't be afraid to call and ask about your pet en route to make sure he's made his flight connections.

Hotel stays are often a necessary part of travelling. Most hotels allow dogs, but many are not explicit in their policies on their websites. If you're booking hotel stays and plan to have your Aussie with you, it is always best to call the hotel to alert them that you have a dog. Some hotels charge pet fees, have limits on how many dogs you can have per room, set aside rooms specifically for guests with dogs, or have you sign an additional agreement to pay for damages should any occur.

Always be considerate of others and respectful of hotel policies concerning dogs. Never leave your Aussie at the hotel unattended, always keep him quiet and properly restrained, and ensure you pick up after him. Some hotels refuse to allow dogs in the rooms after the privilege has been abused by others in the past. Remember, it is your responsibility to care for your dog and keep him under control!

Photo Courtesy of Amanda Glazar

Boarding Kennels vs. Dog Sitters

Sometimes you may need to travel without your Aussie. Boarding kennels and pet sitters are good options to care for your dog while you are away. Boarding kennels offer an assigned area to your dog at their facility and may also offer grooming during stays. Most boarding kennels employ people to feed, exercise, and clean up after your dog and are usually licensed and insured. They also usually require proof of vaccinations, including a kennel cough vaccine.

Pet sitters, on the other hand, can either come to your home or keep your Aussie at theirs. They may only have one or two dogs to care for and can usually offer more personalized care. Good pet sitters are usually harder to find but can be a great option for some dogs, especially those easily stressed by a kennel environment.

Photo Courtesy of Martin Meslo

When considering boarding your Aussie or hiring a sitter, choose carefully. Don't be afraid to interview the business owners or kennel staff caring for your dog. Ask to see the facility or area where your Aussie will be staying. Make note of how they handle and interact with other clients and check online for positive or negative reviews. If at any time you feel concerned or unsure about a situation, trust your gut and look elsewhere. Before leaving your Aussie, it can help to bring him to the kennel facility or allow him to meet and greet the sitter beforehand to make the transition easier.

Traveling with your Aussie and going on adventures together can be a great experience, with many fun memories to cherish. Sometimes we simply can't bring them along with us, however, and for those times it is great to have a trustworthy person or team lined up to take them in for a short time!

CHAPTER 12
Nutrition

"Typically, your breeder will recommend a diet that works best for their dogs. Listen to them."

Melonie Eso
WCK Aussies

A healthy, complete diet is the cornerstone of good health both for dogs and humans. With hundreds of brands of pet foods to choose from, as well as homemade diets, raw diets, wet versus dry food and more, it may seem an overwhelming task to choose which food is best for your Aussie. This chapter will help you to navigate the many choices you have for feeding your new pet.

Photo Courtesy of Lauren Dunning

The Importance of a Good Diet

Dogs are incredibly adaptable creatures and their diet has changed drastically over thousands of years from what it once was. Dogs are descended from wolves, which hunted prey for raw meat and organs to fulfill most of their dietary requirements. As they became domesticated, they adapted to eating what man discarded – slaughter waste, old food, bread crusts, and whatever they could catch or scavenge on their own. The first commercial dog food was not invented until 1860, so kibble is a relatively new addition to dog's diets. Today, most commercial foods follow nutritional guidelines established through studies and feeding trials.

HELPFUL TIP
Cheap Food is Junk Food

Many people feed their dogs the cheapest food they can find, assuming it's as good as anything. That's far from the truth. Cheap dog food is equivalent to fast food for humans. Sure, it will keep you alive, but it's likely to cause health problems down the road. Plus, imagine if you ate greasy cheeseburgers and fries every single day—you might enjoy the taste, but you probably wouldn't feel very good. You're in control of your dog's diet, so feed him even better than you feed yourself to save money on vet bills and extend your dog's life.

Choosing a Quality Commercial Food

Kibble is an affordable, convenient, nutritionally complete diet. One of the easiest ways to determine the quality of a brand is to look at the ingredients on the bag. The closer an ingredient is to the top of the list, the more there is of it in the kibble. So, depending on what you're choosing to feed your dog—whether meat, grains, or vegetables, look for that ingredient to be highest on the list in order to know what your pet is eating the most of. Avoid foods that use generic terms for animal proteins, like "animal fat" and "meat and bone meal". The meat sources in these cases are often questionable at best. The ingredients should always be specific, like "chicken" or "fish meal".

Beware of a tactic called "ingredient splitting". The ingredients list may have named protein sources as the first few listed, but often you can see quite a few different types of grains or legumes listed. This can cause the total amount of animal sourced protein to be much lower than the total

Photo Courtesy of Joanna Feldman

sum of the grains by weight when grouped together.

While dog food, like human food, may be dyed to make it look more appealing to the humans that buy it, dyes are neither necessary for dogs, nor healthy. They can often cause digestive problems such as vomiting and diarrhea in your Aussie. Try to avoid dog foods that have any type of dye in them.

Some dog owners choose to feed canned food over dry kibble. Canned foods contain more moisture, which is more palatable to finicky eaters. The texture is also easier for elderly dogs and young puppies to consume. Again, look at the list of ingredients to determine what your dog is largely eating.

While grain free foods have become a popular choice for many dog owners, mounting evidence suggests that commercial grain-free diets may predispose dogs to canine dilated cardiomyopathy (DCM). More research needs to be done, but many vets are now recommending that pet owners avoid grain-free diets. If your dog needs to remain on a grain-free diet due to allergies or particular food intolerances, your veterinarian may recommend carefully monitoring your dog for symptoms of DCM including lethargy, weight loss, coughing, and more.

Homemade Diets

While most dog owners feed their pets commercial kibble, home-prepared and raw diets are becoming popular. Homemade diets are more time consuming to prepare and can be more expensive in some cases, but dogs with many food allergies often benefit from home prepared meals. The vitamins, minerals, fats, and amino acids are fresher than those found in many commercial kibbles. Care must be taken to ensure your Aussie's complete nutritional needs are being met. Dogs cannot simply be thrown muscle meat and be expected to thrive – they need calcium and other minerals from bones, vitamins from organ meats and small amounts of fruit or vegetables, and so on. Deficiencies usually take time to develop and may be subtle. Therefore, ensure you are feeding a balanced and varied diet over time! Make sure you consult with your veterinarian before implementing any new homemade diet.

There is much controversy surrounding raw food diets for dogs. Many believe that raw food is as unsafe for dogs as it is for people – however, this is a flawed way of thinking. Dogs have very strong immune systems and tough guts. They can completely digest raw bones and can eat a quality raw diet with very low risk of developing foodborne illnesses. A small number of dogs do struggle to digest raw food, or have weaker immune systems due to underlying diseases. These dogs can be fed gently cooked meals, with an alternative source of calcium supplement, as cooked bones are hazardous.

When preparing raw diets, think of a meal in terms of your dog's weight. Adult dogs on average need to consume 2-3% of their bodyweight per day, and puppies need approximately 5%. To ensure your dog's meals are balanced, you can follow this ratio as a general guideline:

- 80% Muscle meat (any muscles, eggs, and certain muscle organs like heart, lungs, gizzard)
- 10% Bone
- 5% Liver
- 5% Secreting organs (kidneys, pancreas, testicles, brain, etc)

Muscle meat includes not only items like chicken breast, ground beef, fish, and roasts but also eggs and muscle organs like heart, lungs, and poultry gizzards. Avoid overly fatty cuts of meat as these can cause stomach upsets.

Raw meaty bones are critical to a healthy diet and clean teeth. Keep in mind that the muscle meat attached to the bones must be counted into the total meat ratio, not the bone ratio. Meat-to-bone ratios for poultry carcasses are typically 30% bone for legs and thighs, and approximately 50% for wings, backs, necks and feet. Beef ribs are 50% while lamb and pork ribs are 30%. Alternative forms of calcium for those feeding cooked diets without raw bones include bone meal, and finely ground eggshells. A general rule of thumb for adding these is a half teaspoon of ground eggs shells or one teaspoon of bone meal per pound of food.

Organ meats are another important part of a balanced diet for your Aussie. Secreting organs like liver, kidneys, brain, pancreas, and testicles provide various vitamins and minerals that bones and muscle meats do not. Liver should always make up half the total organ weight.

Photo Courtesy of
Michelle Mazor

An additional 5-10% of vegetables, fruits, and fresh herbs are also valuable to your Aussie's diet. Wolves and other wild canids typically eat the gut contents of their prey and have been known to be opportunistic scavengers of various vegetation and fruits. Lots of greens, small amounts of berries, and roots or squash rich in vitamins, minerals, and enzymes that are safe and appropriate for dogs are all good choices. Choose a variety and ideally, these should be pureed to aid thorough digestion. Most dogs do not need grains added – if you do, choose higher quality grains like rice or barley and thoroughly soak or cook them before feeding. Keep the amounts small and below 10% of the meal weight. Cases of DCM have not typically been documented in dogs fed homemade raw diets, possibly due to the high amounts of fresh muscle meat supplying additional nutrition to support cardiovascular health.

The benefits of homemade diets are often cleaner teeth, fresher breath, better weight management, and less excrement to pick up as the dog's food is not full of indigestible fillers that bulk up the stool. Many dogs thrive on a well-rounded homemade diet when care is taken to ensure variety over time! Again, make sure you consult your veterinarian before implementing any changes to your dog's diet.

Supplements

While supplements can occasionally be beneficial, remember that too much of a good thing can become problematic. Complete supplements should be avoided for dogs on commercial diets, as they already contain all the nutrients your dog requires. Supplements can be used occasionally for dogs on homemade diets if you are concerned you may not be fully meeting your dog's nutritional needs. Supplements that are typically safe and beneficial for a dog on any diet include fish oils for skin and coat health and probiotics for gut health. Any supplements should be discussed with your veterinarian to ensure the safety of your Aussie.

Treats And People Food

Just like dessert for people, treats need to be limited for your Aussie. Too many treats can offset the balance of his diet, as well as cause obesity. Food can certainly be used as a reward for positive reinforcement training, but the 'rewards' (treats) should be provided in moderation. Also, the same rules apply for treats as for dog food: pick a quality treat, one without any

Photo Courtesy of Tania Gomez Ayala

dyes or propylene glycol. Often-times, your Aussie will be just as happy with a piece of kibble!

Avoid feeding your Aussie people food. This, too, can cause dietary upset and obesity. While a little cheese or a piece off your steak is all right every once in a while, scooping the leftovers on everyone's plate into a dog's bowl after dinner every night is a bad idea. Dogs' digestive systems require routine – sudden dietary changes are likely to make them very sick. There are also some foods that are quite toxic to dogs, which are perfectly harmless to us. These include:

- **Chocolate**

Cocoa contains a bitter alka-loid called theobromine. Dogs struggle to process this com-pound, allowing it to build up to toxic levels in their bodies.

- **Onions and Garlic**

These root vegetables contain compounds that can cause damage to red blood cells.

- **Avocados**

This fruit can cause vomiting and diarrhea.

- **Grapes and Raisins**

These fruits contain toxins that can cause severe kidney damage.

- **Fresh yeast (found in raw bread dough and the like)**

Bread dough and fresh yeast can cause bloating and diarrhea.

- **Fruit cores**

Pits from fruits can cause intestinal obstructions, and many of these as well as apple seeds contain cyanide which can cause severe poisoning.

- **Caffeine and alcohol**

Dogs are more sensitive to the effects of caffeine and alcohol. These can cause severe nervous system disturbances like seizures and comas.

- **Large amounts of foods high in fat (such as milk, cheese, bacon, etc)**

   Fatty foods can cause inflammation of the pancreas, which is life-threatening.

Weight Management

People often think they are being kind by feeding their dogs as much as they want to eat. However, overfeeding can lead to obesity in your Aussie. Just like overweight people, an overweight dog can have problems with the heart, joints, and even develop diabetes among many other conditions. Being overweight can significantly decrease a dog's life span and reduce the quality of its life. Also, one of the first signs of a health issue in your dog is a decreased appetite, and it's hard to tell whether or not your Aussie is eating when everyone in the house is topping off the food bowl throughout the day. One of the first questions your vet will ask you when you bring your dog in for an emergency or illness will be 'how is your dog's appetite? When was the last time your dog ate?'. Your adult dog only needs to be fed an appropriate amount about twice per day.

A dog with an ideal bodyweight should have a slightly tucked waist, and a moderate waistline when viewed from above. When you run a hand over the rib cage you should be able to feel individual ribs with light pressure, covered by a thin fat layer. If you can't feel your Aussie's ribs, he is overweight. If you can clearly feel the outline of his ribs, your dog may be a little thin. Regularly assess your Aussie's body condition and adjust meal sizes accordingly.

Understanding the basics of a healthy diet is extremely important for your Aussie's longevity and quality of life. Whether you choose a commercial kibble or a home-prepared diet, quality counts!

Photo Courtesy of Haley Roberts

CHAPTER 13
Grooming Your Australian Shepherd

"With a good balanced diet, sheds are typically twice a year. Also depends on the climate where you live. You will have hair tufts floating around your house and you will have dog hair on your clothes. Get used to it! The more you groom your Aussie the less of an issue the hair will be."

Melonie Eso
WCK Aussies

While Australian Shepherds certainly shed, their coat was intentionally bred to be low maintenance and weather resistant. Appropriate, regular upkeep will make grooming an easy and pleasant experience for both you and your Aussie!

Photo Courtesy of
Katherine Frantz

Coat Care Basics

Good coat care habits begin with good training. Early on, puppies should begin learning to tolerate gentle brushing, nail trimming, and to allow their ears, mouth, and paws to be handled. Keep the sessions short and fun, rewarding with praise as you pick up a foot or lift an ear or lip for inspection. Dogs who fight grooming are a chore to maintain, and when this happens, coat upkeep often suffers.

The second secret to a coat that is a breeze to maintain is a great diet! Ensure your kibble or homemade diet is excellent quality and nutritionally balanced. Examine your Aussie's skin each week. Does it appear healthy and virtually odorless? Or is it dry, flaking, inflamed, or have a sickly-sweet smell? Dry skin can often be remedied by adding a small amount of quality salmon oil to your Aussie's food each day. This is a high-calorie supplement, so talk to your vet and monitor body weight carefully. Funky, sweet odors exuding from the skin, areas of hair loss, and chronically unhealthy skin can be an indication of allergies, yeast infections, and thyroid issues among other health problems and should always be addressed by a veterinarian.

Never, ever shave your Aussie's coat with clippers. It does not truly reduce shedding, and it does not help him to stay cooler or more comfortable. Shaving double-coated breeds can actually permanently damage the coat, causing it to grow back thin, patchy, or even a different color. Sometimes shaving double-coated breeds can also irritate the skin, causing rashes that can lead to skin infections. Keeping your Aussie's coat intact and maintaining it with the techniques outlined in this chapter is a far better solution for keeping your pup looking and feeling his best!

Bathing and Drying

"They require frequent grooming. As a double coated breed, they need to be brushed well. I also trim their feet, their skirts, ears and back end. Mine love to be blow dried and the brushing is a treat."

Joan Fry
Bella Loma Kennels

Photo Courtesy of
Joshua Martin

Regular bathing and brushing greatly reduces hair left around the house and helps control shedding. This will also help keep your Aussie's skin healthy, will help you to notice any changes in his health, and can often be a bonding experience.

Generally, bathing once every 8-12 weeks is sufficient. The more often you bathe, the more critically important it is to choose a shampoo that is high quality and nourishing to the skin. Often, shampoos marketed to professional groomers tend to be better quality than those sold in the pet aisle at grocery stores. Concentrated shampoos that require dilution often give you more bang for your buck than formulas that are ready to use straight out of the bottle. If your Aussie has allergies or sensitive skin, try using a hypoallergenic formula containing oatmeal.

Test the water temperature before you put your Aussie in the tub – if the water is too hot, you can accidentally burn him. When bathing, know that water temperature matters! Warm water helps release shedding hair, while cool water stalls this process and can help your dog retain his coat. Have towels on hand, and preferably a non-slip mat in the bottom of the tub. Removable shower heads make bath time much simpler, otherwise have a bowl on hand for rinsing. Thoroughly wet the coat from top to bottom. Add a generous amount of shampoo – too much is better than not enough! Massage and work the shampoo into the coat, adding more water as needed. Take care not to get soap or water into your dog's ears or eyes! When rinsing, start again from the top and work your way down, ensuring you are completely removing the soap from each area before moving on. When you have rinsed the entire body, rinse yet again, then feel with your hands to make sure there are no soapy spots remaining – any shampoo accidentally left in the coat can cause intense skin irritation and scratching. Most Aussies do not need a coat conditioner if their skin is healthy, and a good quality shampoo is used. Some canine coat conditioners can weigh down the hair, leaving it feeling greasy or tacky and slow to dry.

When drying your Aussie, allow him to shake some of the water out of his coat first. As you begin toweling him off, gently squeeze the hair with the towel versus rubbing vigorously, particularly where the hair is longer - rubbing tends to create tangles. After towel drying, you can allow your dog to air-dry if you wish or crate him with a box fan blowing on him. However, one of the best ways to control shedding is to employ the use of a force dryer. These high-powered dryers are used by professional groomers to thoroughly strip water and dead hair from the coat. Force dryers for home use are typically between 1HP-4HP. When introducing your Aussie to a force dryer, start slow to get him used to the loud noise, and make sure your pup is secured to a grooming table. Start

Photo Courtesy of
Megan Rogers

on the lowest setting if it is a multi-speed dryer. Facing your Aussie's rear, reach your arm nearest the dog underneath his body and hold him to you. With your free arm, apply the air to the hocks or breeches first and concentrate on this area. Always start from the rear of the dog and work your way forward. Use lots of praise for good behavior, or even small food rewards as they allow you to work with one arm free. Always end on a good note – if your dog is scared or resisting wildly, back off a little until they are calm, then end the session there. Aussies are intelligent and will soon realize that while the dryer is noisy and strange, it is harmless. Be sure to never allow the dryer to blow into your dog's face or ears – generally it is better to finish these areas with a human hair dryer on a cool setting, or allow them to air dry.

Brushing and Tidying the Coat

Brushing is the single most important part of grooming your Aussie. Weekly brushing controls shedding and helps maintain healthy skin by releasing the natural oils it produces and increasing blood circulation. Choosing the correct tools for the job is equally important! Typically, a pin brush and an undercoat rake are all the brushes you'll need. The pin works best for average coat maintenance, while the rake aids in removing dead undercoat during times of heavy shedding. Ensure you are brushing all the way to the skin by using a technique called line brushing.

Begin at the area by the elbow. Using the back of your hand, lift the coat to expose the skin. Start at this line and brush downward, following the grain of the hair. Work in a line from left to right, lifting each section of hair as you go. Then start again just above the first row of hair you completed, repeating this line and moving your way up the rib cage onto the topline and neck. Repeat this technique on each side of your Aussie. This ensures that you are brushing all the way to the skin, removing any dead coat in the process.

Little more is required to maintain an Aussie coat. However, most owners prefer to tidy or trim somewhat, or to neaten up a dog's fringes for the show ring. Straight scissors intended for dog grooming are a necessity for this, and a quality pair of thinning shears can also be handy if you want a more blended look. The areas most commonly trimmed are the feet and hocks.

To trim away excess hair on the feet, lift your Aussie's foot and examine the underside. Using straight scissors, trim any hair sticking out so it is flush with the paw pads. Trim the hair around the edges of the foot, rounding it.

Next, use your pin brush to gently back brush from the tips of the toes towards the leg and trim the excess tufts flush with the top of the foot. For the hocks, brush the hair straight back, and trim as short as you desire.

Some pet owners also choose to shorten the breeches, fringes on the backs of the front legs, the underline (bottom of the rib cage), the ruff (the mane of hair on the front of the neck), and the tops of the ears. While this can be accomplished with straight scissors, generally they leave a displeasing choppy look to the coat. Good thinning shears allow for a much more blended job, although they are more time consuming as they take out less hair with each cut. Simply fluff the hair with your pin brush and trim as short as you desire.

Trimming the Nails

Keeping your Aussie's nails short is essential to his comfort and wellbeing. Long nails can cause pain in the toes, feet, and pasterns and are prone to breaking or even being torn off completely. While this routine care is often intimidating to owners, it does not have to be! Ensure your Aussie is used to having his feet handled. Make this an enjoyable experience and praise your dog when he allows you to hold his foot and wiggle his toes.

To trim your dog's nails, select trimmers intended for dogs. If your puppy is still small, human toenail clippers will work for a little while. Dog nails have a blood-filled center called the quick, with nerve endings that are sensitive when cut. You can avoid hitting them by mistake by knowing where to trim and taking off only small sections of nail at a time. Hold the foot out and trim each nail just where it starts to curl near the end; pink nails often are translucent enough that you can even see the quick in good light. Quicks can also lengthen or recede within the nail. To keep the quicks shorter, keep your dog's nails short!

Many owners prefer to grind their pets' nails as it's difficult to grind the nails short enough to bleed. A nail grinder can also help get nails shorter than traditional trimmers and helps the quick recede faster if it has grown out. Choose a grinder intended for pets with a rechargeable battery. Make sure your dog is secured so he can't wiggle way during the process. You want the leash to be slightly taut when your Aussie is sitting or standing - this will protect him from accidently touching his nose to the grinder. If your dog has long hairs on his toes, it is important to trim these so they do not catch in the grinder.

Hold the foot out and turn on the grinder. Allow your dog to get used to the sound and praise him when he is calm. Pull any remaining stray hairs back with your fingers, hold the intended toe gently but firmly, and apply the grinder for a few seconds to the end of the nail, rounding edges as you go. Check your progress – if you see a small circle or pink, you've ground the nail down as far as it is safe to go.

Ideally, nails should be trimmed or ground weekly to keep them comfortable and the quicks short. If you are truly uncomfortable with this task, talk to your veterinarian or a local professional groomer and schedule regular nail trims for your Aussie.

Cleaning Ears, Eyes, and Teeth

Not only should you manage your Aussie's coat and nails, but his eyes, ears, and teeth need some attention too. Ears can be prone to yeast or bacterial infections and foreign bodies. Examine them weekly and take note of their appearance and odor. Red, warm, moist ears, any excessive substance buildup, or odd smells need to be examined by a veterinarian. Avoid over the counter ear cleaners unless recommended by your veterinarian – some cleaners can irritate the ear canal and make them more prone to infections. To clean the ear of normal dirt or wax, simply take a soft cloth dampened with warm water and gently wipe away the grime only as far as you can see. Do not put anything inside your dog's ears, including q-tips.

Most dogs get a small amount of crusty eye discharge in the inside corner of their eyes, and this is normal. To clean, simply use a damp cloth to gently wipe the area. Note any redness, excessive tearing, thick discharge, or clouding of the eyes and be sure to have any of those symptoms checked by your veterinarian.

Keeping your Aussie's teeth clean is very important to his health. Not only does periodontal disease cause rank breath and extreme discomfort to your dog, but it can also predispose him to heart, kidney, and liver disease as well as jaw fractures. Ensure your Aussie is used to allowing you to touch his mouth from the very beginning. Take his muzzle in your hand and lift his lips gently to examine the teeth, praising him calmly when he cooperates. Note any plaque buildup, or any broken or missing teeth. Cracked or broken teeth and excessive plaque buildup should be seen and remedied by a veterinarian.

Prevent plaque buildup by brushing your dog's teeth two to three times per week. To brush their teeth, choose a toothpaste designed specifically for dogs.

Human toothpaste can be toxic. Some dog toothbrushes slip over the end of your finger to make brushing easier. Secure your dog on a grooming table or in a small room and apply a small amount of toothpaste to the toothbrush. Next, gently lift your dog's lips to expose the teeth and gums. Brush in gentle circular motions, praising your Aussie when they tolerate this. Be sure to reach the back molars. If your Aussie is struggling with having their teeth brushed, keep sessions short but frequent and reward them with affection or play.

To aid in clean teeth, offer a raw beef femur bone or raw frozen turkey neck to gnaw once a week. Your Aussie's instinctual desire to chew will naturally scrape plaque off of his teeth and keep his jaws strong. Only offer raw bones, which are safe for dogs and completely digestible – never cooked or smoked bones, as these are indigestible and prone to splintering.

When Professional Help is Necessary

If you find you are struggling to keep up with thorough grooming and coat maintenance, or you are just overwhelmed during peak shedding season, there are many pet grooming parlors to choose from in most areas. However, be cautious in who you choose. Incompetent or inexperienced groomers could easily stress or unintentionally harm your Aussie. Not all states require that dog groomers be licensed or receive professional training, and the cheaper option may not be the best option!

Talk to your veterinarian and other pet owners in your area to see who they recommend. Check reviews on the internet and social media as well - overwhelmingly positive reviews are a good sign. When you have selected one or two groomers to investigate further, contact them and ask if you can come in for a meet and greet and a tour of the facility. Ask about their prices, policies, years of experience and any training or qualifications

HELPFUL TIP
Shedding Season

Australian Shepherds typically shed their undercoat two to four times per year when the seasons change. Brushing them regularly during shedding season not only helps keep down the amount of hair in your house, but it prevents mats and helps your dog regulate his body temperature.

they may have. When you visit the facility, take note of the environment. Is it calm and reassuring, or tense and bustling? Are the groomers calm and confident around the dogs? Many pets are more stressed and less cooperative when their owners are nearby, so do not be alarmed if a groomer does not allow owners to be present during grooming. They may instead allow you to observe part of the process on another dog.

Remember that it is your responsibility to train your Aussie to allow his feet and body to be touched or handled, not your groomer's. If you are struggling with your dog's behavior in a certain area, consider contacting a professional trainer or certified animal behaviorist to work through any issues before booking an appointment with a groomer. If your Aussie is in urgent need of grooming but is struggling with a negative behavior, be sure to explain the situation to the groomer up front and ask if they would be willing to work through this. Be prepared to pay for more of their time, and to potentially split the session up into several visits to keep it a brief and positive experience for your Aussie.

If you brush your Aussie at least once per week, he may only need to visit a professional for a full groom once every three to six months. If you do not brush him frequently, every four to eight weeks is more appropriate.

Keeping your Aussie looking and feeling his best is a critically important part of his well-being. Regular grooming helps catch many diseases and ailments in their early stages, allowing them to be more readily treated. Grooming is also a bonding time. Whether you do most of the grooming yourself at home, or you rely on a professional, you cannot help but admire this beautiful breed when they are strutting about in a clean, healthy coat with bright eyes and perked ears!

CHAPTER 14
Australian Shepherd Healthcare

"The Australian Shepherd is prone to cataracts, collie eye disease, MDR1 (multi drug sensitivity), hip and elbow dysplasia, epilepsy, and cancer. A good breeder tests for diseases and knows where cancer has occurred in their lines."

Francine Guerra
Alias Aussies

Taking the time to learn to be a steward of your Aussie's health and wellness is an exceptionally important responsibility. Canine healthcare is a broad and seemingly ever-changing topic, and it is up to you to educate yourself in order to make the best possible choices for your Aussie.

Visiting the Vet

Just as you see your doctor annually for a physical examination, so should your Aussie! Regular vet visits can catch many ailments early, when they are easiest to treat. Your vet will check your Aussie's ears, eyes, mouth, abdomen, and genitals, as well as take his temperature and listen to his heart. They may also have you bring in a stool sample to check for intestinal parasites and take a sample of blood to check for heartworms and tickborne diseases. Dogs that are elderly or have known chronic health problems may also need various bloodwork or other tests run regularly, as recommended by your veterinarian.

Photo Courtesy of Eva Kory

Internal and External Parasites

External parasites like fleas and ticks can cause great discomfort for your Aussie, as well as some serious illnesses. Tick bites are prone to causing several different diseases, including Lyme Disease, Ehrlichiosis, Anaplasmosis, Rocky Mountain Spotted Fever, Babesiosis, and Bartonellosis. These diseases require early diagnosis and broad-spectrum antibiotics. Blood tests to check for tickborne illnesses should be run at least every 12 months, especially for dogs that regularly spend time in woods, brush, or fields as they are at higher risk for picking up infected ticks.

Fleas are a problem that can quickly get out of hand if you are not vigilant. These pesky parasites multiply very rapidly and can make your Aussie miserable. Their bites are intensely itchy, and many dogs can develop an acute allergic reaction. Fleas and ticks are most easily controlled by using a synthetic topical or oral pesticide designed specifically for dogs. Topical treatments include Fipronil, Imidacloprid, or Permethrin, while oral drugs include Lufenuron, Spinosad, and Nitenpyram. Be aware that Permethrin is toxic to cats and considered a carcinogen to humans, so perhaps consider other treatments. Some oral drugs are used in combination with those

Photo Courtesy of Courtney Baney

used to treat internal parasites concurrently; however, caution is advised as drug reactions seem to be more prevalent when given all at once. While most of these drugs are generally considered safe, some dogs are more sensitive than others.

Intestinal worms include hookworms, roundworms, tapeworms, and whipworms while other parasites that inhabit the gut, called protozoan parasites, include coccidia and giardia. Intestinal parasites are typically contracted by ingesting their eggs or larva orally from contaminated soil, water, or rodents. The dreaded heartworm, on the other hand, enters the bloodstream via a mosquito bite before taking up residence in the heart.

Symptoms of internal parasites include diarrhea, vomiting, weight loss, dull coat, low energy, and coughing among others. These symptoms require a checkup by a veterinarian, who will check the dog's stool or blood for signs of parasites. There are many different drugs on the market today to treat parasites, including several that are over the counter. However, not all drugs kill all parasites, and in some areas the parasites may have developed resistance to certain drugs. Drugs that are used to treat internal parasites include ivermectin, fenbendazole, praziquantel, and many others. Coccidia requires a different type of drug such as Sulfadimethoxine. Whenever your dog has been treated for internal parasites, follow-up stool samples should be brought to your veterinarian to confirm that the treatment was successful.

Heartworms are of special concern because they are very difficult to treat in their advanced stages and can be lethal. Veterinarians generally recommend a monthly heartworm preventative. Work with your vet to determine which drug will work best for your Aussie, and make sure you understand when and how often it should be administered.

Vaccinations

While there are quite a few vaccines used to prevent many different types of illnesses, not every dog needs every vaccine! Core vaccinations include those against Parvovirus, Distemper, and Rabies. Canine Adenovirus has been considered core as well in years past, however, it has become exceptionally rare in the United States – probably due in part to widespread vaccination. Non-core vaccinations include Parainfluenza, Canine Influenza H3N8, Corona virus, Bordetella (kennel cough), Leptospirosis, and Lyme disease. These vaccines are only given if the risk of contracting the illness are high for your individual dog and their specific circumstances.

Most vaccines are given in a combination dose intended to protect against several diseases all at once. Ideally, less is more. Those that have a higher tendency to cause reactions – specifically, Rabies and Leptospirosis – should be given separately from other vaccines, and not before 16 weeks of age at the earliest for puppies.

Vaccination schedules are more easily understood when you understand how and why vaccines work. Vaccines create immunity to disease by teaching your dog's immune system how to identify and respond to the specific virus or bacteria the dog is being vaccinated against. The bacteria and viruses in the vaccine are killed or weakened and are unable to replicate or cause actual disease. For dogs over 16 weeks of age that have never received a vaccination, most vaccine manufacturers indicate that two doses be given three to four weeks apart to create immunity. Studies have shown that core vaccines, given correctly, can provide up to seven to nine years of immunity. It is now recommended that core vaccines be given no more than every three years, at most, except where a yearly rabies vaccine is required by law.

Young puppies require a slightly different understanding of how their immune systems develop. Newborn puppies receive antibodies from their mother that will protect them for at least five to six weeks. After this point, the maternal antibodies begin to decline. If you vaccinate a young puppy that still has adequate maternal antibodies, the antibodies will render the vaccines useless and prevent the puppy from mounting its own immune response. The idea behind giving puppies multiple vaccine doses several weeks apart until the age of 16-18 weeks is to capture the window where the maternal antibodies still provide some protection but are low enough to allow the vaccine to do its job. Delaying vaccines for too long can mean putting your puppy at risk for disease, while vaccinating too often is a waste

Photo Courtesy of Jordan Kuhl

of a vaccine and stresses your puppy's system. For most puppies, core vaccines given at 8, 12, and 16 weeks of age will adequately protect them.

Vaccinations should always be given by your veterinarian. While very rare, severe anaphylactic vaccine reactions are always possible. These usually occur very soon after vaccination. Your vet will have epinephrine on hand to administer in the off chance this could occur. If such a reaction occurs at home, you may not have time to get your dog to the vet!

Vaccine manufacturers will usually cover medical care in the event your dog contracts an illness that he was appropriately vaccinated against. However, they will only honor this if the vaccination was given by a licensed veterinarian, to ensure that the vaccine was given correctly per the manufacturer's recommendations.

Holistic Alternatives

Many people are becoming increasingly mistrustful of traditional medicine and looking for a more natural way to live – for both themselves, and their pets. There are many things you can do to try a more holistic approach to controlling parasites and managing the risk of disease.

To help control fleas and ticks, ensure your dog is fed a balanced, quality diet and maintains a healthy skin and coat. Clean, healthy dogs are less attractive to fleas, and regular grooming will help catch the beginnings of an infestation or a biting tick early. Whenever you return from an outing where there is tall grass or brush, carefully comb your Aussie all the way to the skin to check for ticks. The ears and face, shoulders, and neck are popular areas for a tick to attach but they can be found anywhere - even between the toes!

Be sure to vacuum regularly underneath furniture and in areas your Aussie likes to lounge. Vacuums are extremely effective at destroying every lifecycle of the flea. You can follow up by lightly applying Diatomaceous earth or an herbal powder designed to kill fleas to your carpet if you happen to see any fleas. Machine washing and drying your Aussie's bedding on the hot cycle is also lethal to fleas. For light flea infestations on your pet, bathe thoroughly with a pet shampoo that contains neem oil and follow this with a vinegar rinse. When bathing a dog with fleas, begin by only wetting and applying soap to the head and ears, then around the base of the tail before applying elsewhere. This is because fleas will attempt to escape by climbing into a dog's nose, ears, etc. Repeat baths one to two times per week until the infestation is eradicated. For more severe infestations, you can also apply 1% Pyrethrin powder to your Aussie's coat every few days until the fleas are under control. Pyrethrin is a natural substance made from chrysanthemum flowers, and while it is quite toxic to fleas, it is well tolerated by dogs. Apply in a well-ventilated area and take care not to get it in your Aussie's eyes or mouth!

Essential oils can also be used as a natural external parasite repellent. Choose a blend of oils like eucalyptus, lemongrass, citronella, lemon, geranium, and cedarwood. Dilute around 5 drops of each in 4oz of distilled water. Shake vigorously before each application and lightly mist your Aussie's coat before walks or hiking.

Internal parasites can be more challenging to control naturally. Ensure you pick up your Aussie's stools promptly and dispose of them in the trash. Do not allow your dog to roam freely in an area where he could happen upon an animal carcass. While some owners choose to deworm their dog monthly, this is not necessary if regular fecal exams come back clear and they don't show any symptoms of internal parasites. Contrary to popular belief, diatomaceous earth has been shown by several studies to be ineffective at eliminating or preventing intestinal worms. Some herbal blends intended for dogs may be of limited use, if given regularly as a preventative measure.

Vaccination is often considered the antithesis of a holistic approach, but in reality a conservative approach to vaccination can go hand in hand with a holistic frame of mind. An alternative to repetitive boosters is vaccine titering. Titers are used to measure your dog's immune response to various diseases. This test can be performed every one to three years to determine which, if any, vaccines should be administered.

While research into the effectiveness of chiropractic care for animals is still rather limited, its benefits are promising. Some pet owners bring their dogs for regular adjustments. It may also be of great help in those animals recovering from injuries. Ideally, look for a veterinarian that is certified in animal chiropractic care.

Homeopathic and herbal remedies have been used for centuries to attempt to prevent and treat every illness or disorder you can think of. While some can be extremely effective, others may be no more than a placebo. If you are considering alternative therapies for your Aussie, be sure to consult with a Veterinary Homeopath or Veterinary Herbalist to determine what remedies will work best.

Spaying/Neutering Your Dog

Reproductive sterilization is the most common way to reduce acciden-tal litters and to help prevent various health problems in your dog later in life. For most pet owners, spaying and neutering is a responsible choice. However, some thought should be given as to when is best to have the procedure done. Studies have shown that spaying and neutering too early, before sexual maturity, can increase the risk of hip dysplasia, cruciate lig-ament tears, and lymphoma. On the other hand, delaying too long can in-crease the risk of mammary cancer in females and prostate issues in males. A happy medium is somewhere between 14 and 18 months, but no earlier than 12 months – this allows your Aussie to finish the majority of his growth while still reaping the major benefits that sterilization offers.

If you choose to delay spaying or neutering your Aussie, it is imperative that you understand your responsibility to prevent accidental litters from occurring. Never allow your dog to roam, and if your Aussie is a female, monitor her carefully for signs of her first heat cycle after six months of age. Signs of heat are moodiness and a swollen vulva, followed by a bloody dis-charge that can last from one to three weeks. If your Aussie goes into heat, keep her away from any intact male dogs for at least three weeks. Never let her out of your sight when outside; she must always be on a leash, and pref-erably behind a fence as well. Male dogs are notoriously good at getting to females in heat. There are panties designed for dogs in heat that your dog can wear while in the house to contain vaginal discharge.

An alternative to traditional spay or neuter surgeries are an ovary-spar-ing spay and a vasectomy. These procedures allow the dog to keep the ova-ries or testicles that provide the hormones necessary to proper growth and development but are completely effective at preventing accidental litters. The downfall of these alternative surgeries is that they are only offered at some veterinary clinics – usually a canine reproductive specialist – and your Aussie will still have the same hormonal tendencies as a dog that is fully intact. However, good training will prevent most problem behaviors from developing.

Common Diseases and Conditions in Australian Shepherds

"Talk to your breeder about health issues; learn what is in the family history and what to expect. There is a wonderful website 'www.ashgi.org' with a ton of great information about health issues in the breed."

Melonie Eso
WCK Aussies

Aussies, like any breed, can be prone to certain genetic health problems. Hip dysplasia is one of the more commonly occurring disorders. This is a painful malformation of the hip joint and is moderately inheritable, although environmental and nutritional factors can also cause or worsen it in some cases. Somewhat less common is elbow dysplasia, a malformation of the elbow joint. Symptoms include pain, stiffness, limping and other gait abnormalities. These conditions can be diagnosed with an x-ray. Ensure your Aussie is fed a balanced diet, and do not allow puppies to do any repetitive jumping or large amounts of endurance exercise before they are fully mature. Never allow your Aussie to become obese, as this puts tremendous strain on his joints.

Several eye disorders affect Australian Shepherds, including Hereditary Cataracts (HC or HSF4), Collie Eye Anomaly (CEA), and Progressive Retinal Atrophy (PRA). Genetic tests can be done to rule out these diseases, although HSF4 is not responsible for all cases of hereditary cataracts. While elderly dogs can certainly get cataracts due to natural aging, true hereditary cataracts most often begin to appear much earlier in the dog's life and can sometimes cause total blindness. Collie Eye Anomaly causes various defects of the tissue of the eye ranging from little or no vision impairment, to total blindness. CEA is apparent in young puppies via an ophthalmologic exam and is non-progressive. Progressive Retinal Atrophy, on the other hand, is a progressive degeneration of retinal tissue leading to blindness and

HELPFUL TIP
Parasites

Ask your vet what parasites are common in your area and keep your dog on a preventative medication all year round. Preventing fleas, ticks, heartworm, or intestinal worms is much cheaper and easier than managing parasites after they've gotten hold of your Australian Shepherd.

can take several years to show up on an eye exam.

Autoimmune diseases are also fairly common in Aussies, and can cause a great deal of misery when severe. This group of disorders occur when the body's immune system begins to attack its own tissues – it can be inherited, but is also often triggered by environmental factors. The most common autoimmune diseases in this breed include moderate to severe allergies, Autoimmune Thyroiditis (hypothyroidism), Inflammatory Bowel Disease, Lupus, and Pemphigus. There is no genetic test for autoimmune diseases, and unfortunately many take several years to develop. Regular visits to your veterinarian will help catch these diseases early.

Photo Courtesy of
Samantha Davenp
IG @coopandtug

Another concern Aussies face is accidental or indiscriminate breeding of two merle dogs. When dogs carry a single merle gene, they display the lovely and unique coat pattern the breed is often known for. However, when offspring inherit two copies of the merle gene – one from each parent – the puppies are often born with large amounts of white. While many people find this striking, it also goes hand in hand with deafness and severe eye defects – some puppies can be born blind, with abnormally small eyes, or no eyes at all.

Cancer is one of the most common causes of death in Aussies, specifically two types of cancer – Lymphoma, and Hemangiosarcoma. The former is cancer of the lymphatic system, while the latter is cancer of the blood vessel walls. Unfortunately, no genetic test or screening exists for these cancers in Aussies. Cancer typically strikes senior dogs (over the age of six). General symptoms include loss of appetite, lethargy, weight loss, and depression. These symptoms should always be checked out promptly by your veterinarian.

Epilepsy strikes fear into the hearts of all who know and love this breed. Many if not most seizures are not caused by true inherited Epilepsy, but a proper diagnosis requires ruling out quite a few other disorders before reaching a diagnosis that is, essentially, the exclusion of all other causes. If your Aussie ever has a seizure, he should receive a full workup by your veterinarian and be carefully monitored. Tragically, there is no genetic test available for breeders to use to reduce the incidence of epilepsy. If you do reach a diagnosis of inherited Epilepsy, please consider participating in the fight against this devastating disease by submitting one of your dog's blood samples to a current canine Epilepsy study.

Of special note is a genetic disorder called Multi-drug Resistance (MDR1), also known as Ivermectin sensitivity. This gene causes dogs to be unable to tolerate certain drugs at levels which are safe for genetically normal dogs. Approximately 50% of the breed carries this gene, which makes it very difficult for breeders to avoid without causing other unintended consequences to the health of the Australian Shepherd's gene pool. The list of active ingredients to avoid includes:

- Ivermectin
- Selamectin
- Milbemycin
- Moxidectin
- Loperamide

- Acepromazine
- Butorphanol
- Chemotherapy Agents
- Emodepside

- Erythromycin
- Vincristine
- Vinblastine
- Doxorubicin

These drugs should never be given to an Aussie that is either known to be a carrier, or that has unknown MDR1 status. Inform your veterinarian that your Aussie is or could be an MDR1 carrier. These drugs can cause seizures, coma, and death; do not be afraid to remind staff and double check to ensure that your Aussie isn't given a problem drug by mistake!

Responsible breeders are on the front lines in the fight to keep this breed as healthy as possible for years to come. Dogs used in breeding programs should have x-rays taken to check for hip and elbow dysplasia, and yearly eye examinations performed by a veterinary ophthalmologist to screen for eye disorders. Many breeders also do a genetic test panel to identify carriers of other diseases.

Problems Aussies are prone to, but for which there are no tests, include epilepsy, autoimmune disorders and allergies, and cancers with a heritable tendency like lymphoma and hemangiosarcoma. If your Aussie is ever diagnosed with any these diseases, be sure to approach your breeder and inform them of the situation. They will need to be aware of these problems to make informed decisions for their breeding program. Responsible breeders also usually have a genetic health guarantee that lasts for several years. No breeder deliberately produces a dog with health problems, and the majority deeply love their dogs and strive to do right by them. Be understanding and courteous – you both want health and happiness for your Aussie!

Pet Insurance

Pet insurance works similarly to health insurance for humans. While routine care is generally affordable, major injuries and illnesses can accumulate high vet bills very quickly. If you opt to purchase pet insurance, start your dog on the plan when he is young as the cost will often be lower. Another reason to opt in sooner than later is that pre-existing conditions are not covered by pet insurance. Don't be afraid to shop around for quotes to ensure you get the best deal possible.

Alternatively, consider creating a savings account where you set aside a monthly amount for your Aussie's care, so that you are prepared in the event of an emergency. Emergencies seem to always pop up in the least opportune moments and you want to make sure you're always well equipped to care for your Aussie's needs.

Understanding basic healthcare for your Aussie is a necessary part of caring for him. From visits to the vet, to preventing external and internal parasites, to understanding the role vaccinations play – you are your Aussie's health advocate! It is up to you to make the choices that are right for your dog and to decide what treatments or preventatives are in your dog's best interest.

CHAPTER 15
Senior Dog Care

The golden years are a special and treasured time in your Aussie's life. You have watched him grow and mature into your best friend and he has become an indispensable member of the family. He may not see or hear as well as he used to, nor be as spry and quick to race to the door to accompany you on a new adventure, but he still loves you as much as he always has.

Basics of Senior Dog Care

Photo Courtesy of Evie Simons

Typically, the senior years begin when a dog reaches seven to eight years of age. Some dogs will age faster or slower than others, but this is the time you can typically start to see some physical and behavioral changes. Keeping senior dogs healthy and comfortable is central to their well-being. Sometimes, this means that changes in your routine and environment must be made to accommodate them.

Some dogs may seem to become grouchy in their old age. In reality, this change in behavior is often caused by various forms of discomfort. Your Aussie's joints may hurt, or he may not see or hear as well as he used to which will put him on edge. Any significant or concerning behavior changes should be seen by your veterinarian to rule out physical or medical causes.

Photo Courtesy of
Mary Stake

Grooming

Grooming days, though perhaps once enjoyed by your Aussie, may become more burdensome for you both. Standing for long periods can become out of the question for elderly dogs with stiff, aching joints. Instead of doing one long grooming session from start to finish, consider dividing it up into several sessions and allow your Aussie to have frequent breaks. You can teach him to allow himself to be groomed while lying on his side. While fringes are beautiful, you may need to consider trimming them shorter to allow for easier maintenance. If you use a professional groomer, consider shorter more frequent visits to make it easier on your Aussie.

When you are grooming your elderly dog, watch for any lumps, new moles, hair loss, or changes in skin color. Some may be harmless age-related changes, while others could signal cancer or other diseases more common in the later years. If your Aussie is beginning to find grooming extremely uncomfortable or even intolerable, or if he seems especially sore the next day, talk to your vet about medications for pain and inflammation.

Nutrition

Many elderly dogs are not as active as they used to be. Their weight can significantly increase, which puts ever more strain on their aging joints. If your Aussie is struggling to maintain a healthy bodyweight, consider switching to a quality, lower calorie food intended for weight management. Alternatively, you can reduce your Aussie's regular meal size and replace that portion with some no-salt -added canned green beans. The fiber will help your dog feel fuller while cutting down on calories.

Supplements that can benefit aging pets include glucosamine and chondroitin, green-lipped mussel powder, and omega 3 fatty acids. These can all support healthy joint function. Some elderly dogs can develop more sensitive guts; a probiotic may help ease problems like gas or loose stools.

Occasionally, elderly dogs may develop medical problems requiring a special diet prescribed by your veterinarian. These could include foods formulated with lower protein for dogs with ailing kidneys, low fat diets for pancreatic disease, and so on. Consult with your vet as to whether your Aussie would benefit from a specific type of diet.

Photo Courtesy of
Cynthia Hokes

Photo Courtesy of Kaity Sevits

Exercise

While motion may be getting more difficult, exercise is still a critical part of your Aussie's health. Australian Shepherds were designed to be in motion! The less mobile your dog is, the faster his body will deteriorate. Regular, gentle exercise keeps muscles and joints strong and improves blood flow. It also helps control weight which will in turn reduce strain on the joints. Appropriate forms of exercise can include walks, swimming, and short games of fetch. Take care to not overdo it – your Aussie does not have the endurance he used to. Even if he seems okay today, he may be sore tomorrow from the overexertion. If you notice your Aussie is sore following exercise, ease up on the intensity and duration next time.

Take note of the temperature outside when exercising your elderly Aussie. Geriatric dogs are more sensitive to heat and cold. Reduce the duration of the exercise during temperature extremes, or keep your Aussie inside for the day.

While your elderly Aussie may not be as spry as he used to be, he is still highly intelligent and will love being a part of whatever activity you're engaged in. Elderly dogs can certainly learn new tricks, and age is no excuse to skimp on your Aussie's mental wellness. Consider taking a class or teaching your Aussie a new game to play to keep his mind sharp! Interactive puzzle games that require your Aussie to work for a treat reward are a great way to entertain them.

Common Old-Age Ailments

As your Aussie ages, he will be more prone to various diseases and ailments. Among the most common is arthritis. Just as in people, a dog's joints begin to deteriorate as he ages. This can result in pain, stiffness, and depression in your Aussie. Veterinarian-prescribed pain medication and joint supplements formulated for dogs can go a long way towards keeping your dog comfortable. Keeping your Aussie's weight down and making sure he keeps moving will help slow the progression of this ailment.

Vision and hearing loss are also quite common as your Aussie ages. You may begin to notice your Aussie doesn't come when you call the first time or run to the door when someone knocks as he can no longer hear it. He may seem clumsy or disoriented if you change the layout of your home as his eyes cannot pick up changes in his environment so easily anymore. Be sure to approach your dog carefully when he is sleeping or unaware of your presence, as he may become frightened when startled and lash out. Use your voice to alert any vision-impaired dog of your presence. For a dog that is hard of hearing, try tapping your foot on the ground to get his attention with the vibrations or gently touch him on the back.

Another unfortunate ailment plaguing older dogs is loss of bowel and bladder control. If your Aussie starts having accidents in the house, be sure to bring him to your vet to check for underlying causes. Sometimes it is simply due to the aging and weakening muscles controlling the bowels and bladder. Your Aussie may need to go out much more frequently or be trained to use a potty pad. Diapers can be worn as a last result, but caution must be used as these can be prone to causing urine scald if your Aussie is not kept very clean and dry.

Heart disease and liver disease are two serious ailments that can affect elderly dogs. Symptoms of heart disease include coughing, fatigue, and

HELPFUL TIP
Managing Arthritis

As your dog starts to limp when the pain of arthritis hits, it may be tempting to limit your Aussie's exercise. While you should limit the intensity of exercise, letting your dog become too sedentary can make arthritis pain worse. Taking your senior Australian Shepherd for several short walks throughout the day will help keep his joints and muscles limber and help prevent as much stiffness and pain from setting in.

shortness of breath. Kidney disease signs include vomiting, lethargy, and increased thirst. If your Aussie is exhibiting any of these symptoms, he should be seen by a vet promptly.

Cancer is one of the most common causes of death in dogs. There are many different forms of cancer affecting near-

STORY
Pockets

The oldest dog in AKC history to earn a title was Australian Shepherd Pockets, who earned the Rally Novice title at the age of 15 years and five weeks

ly every tissue in the body, but a few symptoms of certain types of cancer include lumps and bumps under the skin, abdominal swelling, sores that refuse to heal, changes in appetite, and depression. Some cancers are treatable with surgery, while others have no cure and require that your dog simply be kept comfortable.

Regular veterinary visits are crucial to keeping your elderly dog healthy and comfortable for as long as possible. Blood work should be run yearly to check for signs of underlying disease. Take this time to discuss any changes in health or behavior with your vet, as these could signal health problems brewing.

When It's Time to Say Goodbye

End of life for your beloved companion is a topic few want to think about, but some consideration should be given to this heart wrenching, inevitable event. Many owners struggle with finding the right time to say goodbye. Consider your Aussie's health and happiness – is he still having more good days than bad? Does he still eat well and seem to enjoy life? Are you still able to keep him reasonably comfortable? If the answer to any of these questions is "no", it may be time to consider euthanasia. Speak with your vet to determine if there is anything you can do to improve your Aussie's quality of life.

Try not to wait until your Aussie is truly miserable. When the bad days are becoming as frequent as the good ones, consider choosing one of those really good days and make it a special last day. Take your Aussie out for ice cream, take him to the park, take time to do whatever it is your Aussie loves the most and make some memories. Get some photos of you together so that you have them to cherish.

Sometimes your dog may decline so rapidly that you are left with no other reasonable option than to rush him to the vet. Either way, when it is time, no one wants to make the difficult decision to end the life of a suffering pet...but it takes a courageous and loving owner to do what is best for their beloved Aussie, even if that means saying goodbye. When the time comes, your vet will take you and your Aussie to a private room. You will be able to stay with your Aussie and cuddle or hold them, which will be comforting to them. Your vet will explain what they are doing for each step and why. Typically, a sedative is given that puts your Aussie into a deep sleep within fifteen minutes. After this, your vet will give a lethal injection that causes their breathing and heart to stop within a few minutes. They may have some muscled twitching or other symptoms from the euthanasia drug, but this is a normal process as their body's systems shut down and they are not in any pain or discomfort.

When your Aussie passes on, thought will need to be given for their remains. While many owners bury their pets in their backyard, this may not be the best option and may not even be legal in your location. If you decide to bury them, they must be laid to rest three feet under the ground to ensure that wildlife will not scavenge their remains.

Another option is cremation, where their remains are incinerated and the ashes returned to you. This method is more environmentally friendly and allows you to place your Aussie's remains in a decorated urn to either keep or bury. Some artisans that blow glass specialize in making beautiful pendants or sculptures infused with the ashes, which can become treasured keepsakes.

Finally, depending on the cause of death or euthanasia, you may be able to donate your Aussie's body to canine health research. Speak to your vet about the possibility and whether there are any universities that may be able to take them. In a way, your Aussie will be helping dogs everywhere by providing valuable information to scientists and researchers.

Sharing life with an Australian Shepherd is a journey and a privilege. This breed has an incredible amount of character, and it is no wonder that those who know Aussies well love them so dearly. At times we fall short of being the person they need us to be. Thankfully, they forgive us, and love us just the same. Aussies can be time consuming to raise, but their expressive, intelligent gaze, happily wiggling stub tail, and ready-for-anything attitude makes every minute worth it.

Made in the USA
Monee, IL
04 May 2021